FLORA BRITANNICA BOOK OF
WILD HERBS

FLORA BRITANNICA BOOK OF
WILD HERBS

RICHARD MABEY

Supported by Common Ground

With photographs by
Bob Gibbons and Gareth Lovett Jones

CHATTO & WINDUS
London

First published 1998

© Richard Mabey 1998

Richard Mabey has asserted his right under the
Copyright, Designs and Patents Act 1988 to be
identified as the author of this work

First published in the United Kingdom in 1998
by Chatto & Windus
Random House, 20 Vauxhall Bridge Road,
London SW1V 2SA

Random House Australia (Pty) Limited
20 Alfred Street, Milsons Point, Sydney,
New South Wales 2061, Australia

Random House New Zealand Limited
18 Poland Road, Glenfield,
Auckland 10, New Zealand

Random House South Africa (Pty) Limited
Endulini, 5A Jubilee Road, Parktown 2193,
South Africa

Random House UK Limited Reg. No. 954009

A CIP catalogue record for this book is available
from the British Library

Papers used by Random House UK Limited are
natural, recyclable products made from wood
grown in sustainable forests. The manufacturing
processes conform to the environmental
regulations of the country of origin.

ISBN 1-85619-723-9

Printed and bound in Singapore
by Tien Wah Press

CONTENTS

INTRODUCTION

WE ARE BECOMING so accustomed to the constant stream of wild plants currently being taken into cooking and medicine that it is easy to forget that many of these represent rediscoveries. All cultivated plants had, of course, wild ancestors, and investigating the properties of these as potential food (or poison) marked the first cultural contact between humans and the plant world. A herb could be said to be any plant which passed the test. One traditional definition is that 'herb' is 'applied to plants of which the leaves, or stems and leaves, are used for food or medicine, or in some way for their scent or flavour'. Looking at the immense range of useful plants today, this definition would have to be broadened to include flowers and roots as well as stems and leaves, plants used as detergents and dyes, and the raw material of people as far removed as historic gardeners and holistic healers.

This volume derives from contributions made to *Flora Britannica*, a nationwide project to determine where wild plants stand in our cultural, social and domestic lives – whether, in short, we still have a living botanical folklore.

In Britain, wild plants have traditionally had a central role in folklore. We pick sprigs of heather for luck, munch blackberries in autumn, remember Wordsworth's famous lines when the wild daffodils are in flower, and link hands around threatened trees. Our children still make daisy chains, whack conkers and stick goosegrass stems on each other's backs. Despite being one of the most industrialised and urbanised countries on earth, we cling to plant rituals and mystical gestures whose roots stretch back into prehistory: holly decoration for the winter solstice, kisses under the mistletoe, the wearing of red poppies to commemorate the casualties of war. We name our houses, streets and settlements after plants, and use them as the most prolific source of decorative motifs on everything from stained glass to serviettes. From the outside, it must look as if we are botanical aboriginals, still in thrall to the spirits of vegetation.

Alexanders at Church Knowle, Dorset. Probably a Roman introduction originally, as a pot-herb, it is now thoroughly naturalised, especially (as here) near the coast.

But is this just the dying stages of an obstinate habit, the outward signs of a longing for the rural life that most of us have lost, or is it something deeper? Do we really still believe in the bad luck that may-blossom can bring into a house, and in the efficacy of the increasing numbers of herbal nostrums crowding onto our chemists' shelves? Or is our seeming respect now a touch tongue-in-cheek? When wild flowers are dragged willy-nilly into shampoo advertisements and state rituals, maybe it is time to ask whether the particular plants themselves have any meanings left for us, or whether they have become purely notional, registers of a fashionably Green 'life-style'.

When the survey work on *Flora Britannica* started, this was the question that underpinned all others. We were aware of surviving crafts and cottage wisdom, and of the familiarity expressed in our immense legacy of vernacular plant names. What we did not know was whether, as a people (or collection of peoples), we could be said to have an intimacy with plants that was more than purely nostalgic and backward-looking. Did people still meet under meeting-place trees? Were children inventing new names and games for the new, exotic species constantly escaping into the wild, as they did centuries ago, say, for horse-chestnut and sycamore seeds? And was that two-way traffic of wild and cultivated plants over the garden wall still busy? Did plants continue to play any role in our senses of place and season, those fundamental aspects of everyday life that seem everywhere to be under threat from regimentation and the ironing out of local differences? How had the attractions of wild food and native herbal remedies survived into the era of convenience food and prescription medicines?

These were the kind of questions which were asked when *Flora Britannica* was launched in the winter of 1991–2. Over the four years that followed, the project was regularly publicised on television and in the press, as well as through schools, community groups and amenity societies (more than a hundred of these at local and national levels). The many thousands of responses came in all manner of forms – postcards, tapes of discussions, snapshots and family reminiscences, as well as long and detailed essays on the botanical folklore of individual parishes and individual species.

Those responses that concerned the culinary and medicinal uses of our wild plants form the backbone of this current book.

A note on the text

The text includes species of flowering plants from England, Scotland and Wales. Ireland and the Channel Isles are not included. The species are to some extent self-selected by whether they have figured in local culture and whether contributors reported this. By British botanical standards there is an unusual number of introduced and naturalised species, which are often found more interesting and which, of course, began with a cultural profile, often by already being in trade or in cultivation.

The vernacular names (indicated as 'VN') are all ones that were contributed to the project as being in current use, and they are normally printed in the spellings in which they were submitted. I have tried to eliminate obvious copying from previous printed sources, though there are inevitably some borderline cases. Except in special circumstances, I have not indicated particular areas where particular names prevail. The geographical mobility of contributors, who are often writing from one place and remembering another, and the mobility of the names themselves through the mass media, would have made this a misleading and potentially inaccurate qualification.

The notes from contributors are printed as they were sent in. Editing has been confined to selection of passages and occasional changes in spelling and punctuation to assist clarity. Editorial additions are indicated by square brackets. As many of the contributions were handwritten, I must apologise if I have made any errors of transcription either in the text itself or in the names of contributors.

Reference numbers refer to the Source notes section, which starts on page 150. Contributors are referred to in this section by name, parish and county.

Wild Greens

Edible leaves are just a special category of herb.
Indeed many favourite edible green plants were once
harvested chiefly for their medicinal powers.
Stinging nettle was used as a remedy for colic (and its
fibres for making cloth) before it became a stock
ingredient for soups. Water-cress was once included
in a spring tonic. And it is easy to imagine the

transition between potion and flavouring in plants such as the mints, which made very pleasant drinks in their own right. These days the division is closing again and many green herbs which are used principally as foods or flavourings – for example, thyme, dandelion, fennel – are having their medicinal potentials rediscovered.

Water-cress, common but often contaminated in the wild by liver-fluke larvae. Cooking kills them.

'**Wild foods**'. Since the mid-1970s, foraging for wild plant foods has become almost as common in Britain as on the continent. Even mushroom-hunting has ceased to be regarded as an outlandish and dangerous eccentricity, and you must be out very early in British woods these days to be sure of getting your share of the first ceps and chanterelles. Fortunately the practice has lost most of its early and sometimes over-hearty associations with survivalism and (though it can reduce your food bills) its more fantastical links with self-sufficiency. Foraging is now simply fun, indulged in for the pleasure of new taste experiences, for insights into the history of our cultivated foods, and for more intimate and sensuous encounters with growing things. It can even be rewarding done as little more than wayside sampling: a wild red currant here, a sweet cicely seed there – what the 1930s fruit gourmet Edward Bunyan described delightfully as 'ambulant consumption'.

Since the late 1980s wild plants have also begun to make a perceptible impact on the commercial food business. In France, which has rather more raw materials at its disposal, there is a distinct school known as *cuisine sauvage*. And in Britain it is now not uncommon to find samphire, nettles, dandelions, bitter-cress, borage, wild strawberries, bilberries and ramsons served in some form or other in both smart metropolitan restaurants and local pubs. Perhaps most encouraging is the fact that they are no longer regarded simply as rough peasant foods, but are being used as ingredients for modern *styles* of cooking: wild herbs and fruits flavour-

Sweet chestnuts are sweetest after the first frosts.

ing oils and vinegars (and even Danish-style schnapps); spring greens – garlic mustard, nettle, sorrel – stir-fried; flowers added to salads. A contribution from a Hampshire woman of American ancestry illustrates the inventiveness of the modern approach to wild foods:

'I take so many of these foods for granted that I often forget that many people don't eat such things as dandelion pasta, nettle gnocchi, wild garlic and cheese soup or dandelion and mozzarella pie! I guard any dandelion greens that spring up in my garden with as much enthusiasm as some look after their most prized tomato plants. My latest invention is to chop a load of assorted greens I've gathered, sauté them with garlic and onion, fold in ricotta cheese, some fine bread crumbs and an egg and use this as a stuffing for pasta shells or home-made ravioli … My grandmother's cousin, Amber, had all her workmates gathered round the bench in the mill one day to sample her dandelion and mozzarella pie. She had layered cooked dandelion greens, cheese, sliced black

Winter-cress, an early-flowering species.

Marjoram, the oregano of Mediterranean countries and a common summer-flowering herb of chalk country.

olives and a little tomato sauce made with garlic into flaky pastry and baked it into a pasty. It became her favourite lunch-box treat ... Have you ever had pickled greens? They are wonderful. Mustard greens, turnip greens, wild greens, the patient and persistent dandelion greens – all potted up in a spiced, slightly sweet vinegar. They make a cheese sandwich sing.' [1]

Common nettle or **Stinging nettle**, *Urtica dioica* (VN: Devil's plaything, Hokey-pokey, Jinny nettle). The nettle has given its name to nettle rash (urticaria), to a state of general pique or irritation, and – out of exasperation or respect at its profusion – to at least half a dozen villages in England, including Nettlebed (Oxfordshire), Nettlecombe (Dorset), Nettleham and Nettleton (Lincolnshire), and the Nettlesteads (in Kent, Surrey and Suffolk).[2] A plant which grows in such close, copious and aggressive proximity to human settlements was never in danger of being ignored.

Stinging nettles' natural habitat is fertile, muddy, slightly disturbed ground, especially amongst the lush herbage of silt-rich river valleys and woodland glades manured by feeding animals. Above all, it needs soils rich in phosphates, which is why it has flourished in the wake of human and agricultural colonisation. Human settlements provide phosphates in abundance, in cattle-pens, middens, bonfire sites, refuse dumps and churchyards. Soil-borne phosphates can endure for exceptionally long periods, and ancient nettle clumps (often with other phosphate-lovers such as elder and cleavers) mark the sites of many deserted villages, Little Gidding in Huntingdonshire for instance, and isolated Scottish crofts: 'In the Highlands, ruined crofts occur in very remote places, miles from anywhere. One thing they always have in common – a patch of nettles, even though there are no other nettles for 20 miles in any direction.' [3]

The wooded sites of Romano-British villages on the Grovely Ridge near Salisbury are still dense with nettles subsisting on the remains of an occupation that ended 1,600 years ago.[4] And modern Wiltshire is scarcely any different. Fertiliser run-off from its vast arable prairies has made the county a paradise for nettles, especially along the upper reaches of the River Kennet. In summer a thirteen-and-a-half-mile stretch is an almost continuous double ribbon of nettles (or a broad single swath where the channel has dried out), up to eight feet high. They spread by seed and by means of their tough yellow roots, which as well as extending up to 20 inches a year, are broken off and churned into the mud by cattle, and sluiced further downstream by the river water.[5]

Such an abundance of tender greenery, stings notwithstanding, has been a tempting source of food since prehistoric times. The Romans certainly ate nettles as well as manuring them. On the Celtic fringe they have traditionally been eaten in a kind of soup with oatmeal;[6] and a recipe for St Columba's broth (the sixth-century Irish monk and poet) survives to this day and tastes remarkably like soup made from young peas: 'Pick young stinging nettles before the end of June, when they are 4 or 5 inches high – one handful for each person. Boil, drain, chop and return to pan with water and milk. Reheat, sprinkle in fine oatmeal or oats, stirring until thick. For present-day tastes eat with toast and grated cheese, or peeled soft-boiled egg.'[7]

Nettles have frequently been returned to as a subsistence food, for example during the Irish potato famine of the 1840s and during the Second World War. Ambrose Heath, in his *Kitchen Front Recipes and Hints* (1941), had extravagant praise for both nettle and dandelion leaves: 'A poached egg on a bed of dandelion or nettle purée covered with cheese sauce is an almost perfect meal, containing every one of the foods which we are being told to eat, body-building, protective and energising.' Modern cooks have deep-fried nettle leaves to the texture of green crisps, and used them raw in purées. The distinguished chef Anton Mosimann blends his with fromage blanc, new potatoes and nutmeg into a 'nettle nouvelle'. A woodman from Bedfordshire has a more earthy technique: 'I sometimes make a sort of green vegetable pâté by picking tender nettle tops and smashing them up in a pestle and mortar (which in my case means half a brick and an oak log). I add a mixture of herbs including crushed garlic … wrap it in a lettuce leaf and eat it as a snack.'[8]

A Devon boy ate untreated nettle leaves at school, a trick that echoes 'grasping the nettle' (in which the stem or leaves are gripped quickly and tightly, so that the toxin-laden hairs are crushed before they can pierce the skin): 'The trick is to

Young stinging nettles – here growing by the old Roman Wall at Silchester, Hampshire – are used in soups in the spring.

roll them up in a special way with the tongue, making sure that there is plenty of saliva to coat them.'[9]

'Many years ago a gypsy arrived at my farm asking for scrap … After he had loaded his van his hands were filthy, covered with grease, dust and more than a little cow-dung. Without a word he went to the nettle patch and grabbed a plant and stripped off the leaves – just in one movement. I was fascinated, because of course nettles sting. "How can you do that?" I asked. "Finest thing in the world for cleaning the hands," he said. "And what's more you'll never see a gypsy with arthritis." '[10]

The idea of using nettle stings as a counter-irritant, to 'warm away' inflammations, has some roots in sympathetic magic, but it also has a degree of practicality. According to the Elizabethan antiquary William Camden, the Romans, well aware that Britain would be cold, brought their native nettle with them to rub on their skins. ('Roman nettle', *U. pilulifera*, occurred as a casual in some parts of Britain until the 1950s, but if the Romans did resort to therapeutic self-flagellation they would have found English nettles just as efficient and rather more available.) In the Isle of Man the same custom persisted until quite recently: 'It is widely known as "Jinny Nettle" on the island. The Manx name *Undaagah* comes from an old Gaelic word meaning "flaying", because of the plant's blistering effect on the skin. It was used on the island to restore circulation by beating the skin with it.' [11]

'Both my mother and I use this plant on any joint which gives painful symptoms. The treatment is simple – sting the joint liberally with the plant, and if possible move the joint well immediately after application, e.g. go for a walk. Some relief is felt within 30 minutes, but the gently tingling warmth is felt for many hours. The following day, should any pain in the joint persist, sting again, and eventually full and pain-free movement returns.' [12] The use against arthritis has been to some extent vindicated by the modern medical practice of using bee-venom for inflamed joints.

Using nettle switches rather more recklessly was part of a children's ritual on Oak Apple Day, 29 May, which

Stinging nettle in flower.

seemed to be confined to villages close to the Derby-shire–Staffordshire border between Mayfield and Tansley: '[When I was a girl] in Derbyshire in the 1930s, Oak Apple Day was marked by a special ritual. On the way to school in the morning, the boys armed themselves with sprays of net-tles, and custom licensed them to use the nettles to sting the bare legs of girls unless they carried a safety talisman of a sprig of oak leaves. Such a sprig guarded the girl com-pletely.' [13] In Mayfield itself, boys were just as liable to get 'nettled': 'Stinging nettles, usually about 30 to 40 cm long, were plucked, either using your handkerchief to wrap round the stalk to protect your hands if you were "soft", or using your bare hands if you were "tough", and then used to lash other children across their bare legs (all primary school boys wore short trousers in those days). There was no particular Royalist sentiment in this at that time. It was just a rather sadistic game, although we were aware of the origins.' [14] (Also in Derbyshire, I have heard of a similar spartan application by a farmer's wife who used a nettle switch to get a brood of children out of bed.)

Nettles have also been used to make green manure, by steeping them in rainwater (cf. comfrey, p. 119), [15] and have a long history of use as a fibre in string- and cloth-making. In Britain a flint arrowhead has been found attached by nettle fibres to fragments of its shaft; and remains of nettle fabric were discovered in a Danish grave from the late Bronze Age, wrapped around cremated bones. [16] Nettle-cloth (the fibrous stems treated in much the same way as flax) was cer-tainly manufactured in Scotland and Scandinavia into the early nineteenth century. When Germany ran short of cot-ton during the First World War, it resorted to nettles to make military clothing. Something like two and a half mil-lion kilograms were gathered from the wild, though it took 40 kg to make a single shirt. During the Second World War, some work was done in Britain on the possibility of using nettles in the same way, but in the end the plants were chiefly used for extracting chlorophyll, and as a dye for camouflage nets. [17]

Fat-hen, *Chenopodium album* (VN: Muckweed, John O'the Nile). This common weed of cultivated ground was once a valued crop – a prehistoric staple, probably. It is not difficult to see how it rose to this status. It forms pale green,

mealy-leaved swarms close to human settlements, particularly where rubbish is thrown out – in middens and stack-yards in the Iron Age; today, in muck-heaps at the edges of fields and between the rows of well-dunged crops (ironically, often its domesticated relatives such as spinach and sugar-beet). Early people would not have been slow to try such an accessible and abundant vegetable (especially as it

Fat-hen growing as a weed in Norfolk, ironically amongst its cultivated relative sugar-beet.

has large, fatty seeds) and would not have been disappointed. The whole plant, eaten raw or cooked, is as pleasantly tangy as kale or young broccoli.

Fat-hen is one of those plants whose remains have been found all over Europe in prehistoric settlements. It was part of the last, possibly ritual meal of Tollund Man, the 2000-year-old corpse found in a peat-bog in Jutland in 1950. He had been hanged, either as a punishment or as a sacrifice, and thrown into the bog, where the acid peat in effect pickled him. His last meal was a gruel that included the seeds of fat-hen, gold-of-pleasure, black-bindweed, wild pansy, barley and linseed.

Fat-hen seems to have been important or plentiful enough in some areas to have whole settlements named after it. Its Old English name was *melde*, and the place-name specialist Eilert Ekwall believed that Melbourn in Cambridgeshire, for instance – Meldeburna in 970 – was the stream on whose banks *melde* grew.[18] Later place-name experts would not be so confident. But the association with dung has persisted in surviving local names. In Shropshire it is still known as 'muckweed', but also, more obscurely, as 'Jack (or John) O'the Nile' – or 'nail', which would be pronounced 'nile' in the Midlands.

'I came into the area some 50 years ago when hand weeding behind a horse scuffle was paramount. My first job was weeding sugar-beet (at two shilling and sixpence a week, plus keep) and John O'Nile was the name used by the wagoner, who had no doubt it was "Nile" not "nail".'[18] (But 'nail' does fit with another cryptic Shropshire vernacular name, 'Johnny O'Needle'.)

Deciphering the origins of plant and place names is notoriously full of pit-falls. But in the small farming village of Milden in Suffolk – Meldinges in *c.* 1130 – some villagers have no doubt about the *melde* root of their settlement's name. In the 1970s they commissioned a local blacksmith to make a six-foot-tall cast-iron statue of a fat-hen plant and placed it on a fieldside road-verge on the boundary of the parish. It must be one of the most bizarre – and ambivalent – village signs in the country: a memorial to a dung-hill weed that quite likely gave the settlement its name, sited just yards away from drifts of the real plant, which modern Milden farmers are forever trying to drive out of the fields.

Good-King-Henry, *Chenopodium bonus-henricus* (VN: Mercury, Mercree). For a plant often classed as a weed, Good-King-Henry is surprisingly handsome – upright, shapely and with triangular, sometimes red-tinged, leaves. It is almost always found close to habitation in similar positions to fat-hen, in the rich soils of stackyards, hedge-banks, cultivated ground and rubbish-tips, and it may well have been first introduced as a crop plant by Bronze Age settlers from southern Europe. It is a rather bland-tasting but pleasantly textured green vegetable, undergoing a revival in modern herb gardens.

*Milden's village sign commemorating its name plant, fat-hen (*melde *in Old English), which was once a staple food-plant.*

The name is an anglicised version of the German *Guter Heinrich*, 'Good Henry' (Henry being a Teutonic elf rather like our Robin Goodfellow). The 'Bad Henry' with which the name is meant to contrast is dog's mercury (see p. 134), a poisonous species whose form is vaguely similar to a young *Chenopodium*.[20]

Other goosefoots can be used as pot-herbs, as can most of the closely related oraches. **Garden orache**, *Atriplex hortensis*, probably from Asia, is increasingly grown as a leaf vegetable and occasionally escapes to the wild. **Common orache**, *A. patula*, and **spear-leaved orache**, *A. pros-*

Another edible goosefoot, sea-beet (an ancestor of cultivated beets), on dunes in north Cornwall.

trata, are native species of waste and disturbed ground. **Grass-leaved orache**, *A. littoralis*, and **frosted orache**, *A. laciniata*, are quite common along sandy coasts throughout Britain.

Sea-purslane, *A. portulacoides*, is another coastal species, but a much more distinctive plant. In summer, its mealy, silvery leaves provide one of the key tones in the chequer of pastel greys, greens and purples that cover the upper reaches of saltmarshes on the south and east coasts. It has a particular liking for the edges of small patches of salt water, and 'a bird's-eye view of an east-coast marsh would show nearly every little creek bordered with a light grey band produced by these plants'.[21] Sea-purslane prefers well-drained soils, and the development of these characteristic fringes comes about when the tide overflows the edges of pools and creeks, depositing silt amongst the plants growing on their edges. As a result, the level of the bank is gradually raised above that of the marsh. And as the ground becomes higher and better drained, so the sea-purslane grows more luxuriantly, and eventually blankets out other species.

The leaves make an excellent, crisp ingredient for salads.

Sea-beet, *Beta vulgaris* ssp. *maritima* (VN: Sea spinach, Wild spinach). A large-leaved, straggly perennial which grows on sea-walls, shingle and waste ground on most parts of the coast, except in northern Scotland. It is obviously a close relative of cultivated beets such as Swiss chard, mangel-wurzel, sugar-beet and beetroot, and specimens with red-veined leaves, of the kind developed into beetroots, are quite common in the wild. The leaves are tangy and substantial cooked as a spinach, and one of the most popular of wild vegetables.[22]

Common glasswort or **Marsh samphire**, *Salicornia europaea*, and related species (VN: Samphire, Sanfer, Sandforth). Marsh samphire is *not* the wild vegetable whose gathering Shakespeare described in *King Lear* as a 'dreadful trade'. (That is the cliff-growing rock samphire, *Crithmum maritimum*.) It is a plant of the muddiest zones of saltmarshes, and collecting it is more a draggled than a dreadful business. But it is a special plant, and many people's introduction to the lesser-known reaches of wild-food gathering. It has an aura not shared by many other edible wildings, which comes home most strongly when you see that it is

Marsh samphire, an early coloniser of bare mudflats, and one of the best wild vegetables.

sold (e.g. in Sussex)²³ in fishmongers, alongside the cod and cockles, rather than in greengrocers with the 'land' vegetables. In King's Lynn, Norfolk, it is hawked around the streets by a local picker with a horse and cart, who already has a 'traditional' street-cry: 'Any samphire, you ladies?'

It occurs right around the coast of Britain, but East Anglia is where it is best known and most widely used, and the area which has accumulated the richest lore about the species. North Norfolk is where I first made its acquaintance in the 1960s, as a shiny, succulent plant, rather like a plump, jointed pipe-cleaner, which appeared on areas of bare mud and the edges of creeks from late May onwards. I soon learned that picking shouldn't really begin before the longest day, and that the healthiest specimens were those

'washed by every tide'. There were other, more dubious traditions. The samphire was once pickled by filling jars with the chopped shoots, covering with spiced vinegar and leaving in the local baker's oven as it cooled off over the weekend.[24] What its condition was like afterwards one can only guess.

In those days samphire was gathered when it was about six to nine inches high by being pulled up by the roots. This is now illegal, under the Wildlife and Countryside Act, except with the landowner's permission, and it is more responsible (and time-saving in the long term) to cut the tender tops of the plants with scissors. The stems can be eaten raw as a crisp and salty salad plant, or boiled briefly like thin asparagus and dipped in molten butter or warm oil. They are eaten traditionally by holding the root-end and drawing the stems between the teeth, to strip the flesh off the central spine.

Shrubby sea-blite, a local shrub of east- and south-coast shorelines.

Samphire will keep for a few days, provided it is dry. Left damp after washing, it rapidly wilts – as it does if the roots or cut ends are stood in fresh water, which sucks the sap out of the plant. Samphire's succulence, which is the source of its tangy savour, redolent of iodine and sea breezes, is a biological adaptation to enable it to survive in a salt-water environment. The plant contains sodium salts in solution, to balance the 'sucking' (osmotic) pressure of the sea and prevent the plants being dehydrated. The concentration of salts is so high that they were once used in the making of glass and soap (hence the name 'glasswort'). The plants were dried, and then burnt in large heaps. The ash was heated with sand until it fused into a crude glass, or leached with limewater to make a solution of caustic soda. This was evaporated and the resulting crystals of caustic soda (sodium hydroxide) were used to make better-quality glass or heated with animal fats to make soap.

Lancashire is another samphire centre: 'Pickled samphire is popular in Wigan. Special journeys used to be made by Wigan people to collect samphire from the Ribble marshes in September.'[25]

In other parts of Lancashire, samphire was known as 'sandforth' and gathering the plant as 'sandforthing'.[26] (A friend of mine, accustomed to the Norfolk name and pronunciation and never having seen it written down, used to spell it 'sandfire', which is a wonderful description of the plant in autumn as the tips turn a tawny-red over the flats.)

Samphire is moving up-market now. It had an honoured place in the wedding breakfast of Prince Charles and Diana in 1981, delivered fresh from the Sandringham Estate in Norfolk; [27] and it appears increasingly on the menus of smart restaurants, though sometimes just as a garnish for fish, like a maritime parsley (and often commercially imported from Brittany).

Its distribution and abundance are also constantly changing. The annual species (which are highly variable, with 20 to 30 'sorts' distinguishable in south-east England)[28] are amongst the earliest colonisers of fresh, bare estuarine mud. They can grow as thick as grass in the first few years, forming samphire 'lawns', but decline as the mud stabilises

and perennial saltmarsh species move in. In East Anglia, samphire's *locus classicus*, it may actually be increasing. The Eastern coastline is slowly sinking as a result of natural earth-movements and the warming of the sea, flooding more drained land each year and opening up new samphire sites all the time.

There is a story that in 1953, after the terrible east-coast floods, a monster samphire plant, six feet tall, was found in a creek near Blakeney in north Norfolk. It was strapped to a bicycle crossbar, taken to the local pub and hung above the bar like a prize fish. Forty years later I saw a more credible development for myself, in a creek in much the same place. A crumbling plastic dinghy, moored a few yards off-shore, was carrying the remains of a presumably self-sown crop of samphire. I had a vision of the owners using it like an out-size maritime equivalent of one of those mustard-and-cress cartons, towing it in for the occasional snip in season, and then setting it adrift again.

Shrubby sea-blite, *Suaeda vera*, is a scarce evergreen shrub which forms dense, scrubby colonies on some beaches and the upper reaches of saltmarshes on the south and east coasts of England. It is a species with a distinctly Mediterranean distribution in Europe, yet it seems perfectly adapted to the often turbulent conditions of the North Sea coast. In shingle that is tossed about by winter storms it grows with a low, creeping habit, which allows the stems to become buried under the shifting stones. New shoots then sprout from the submerged stems, even when they are two or three feet below the surface.

Shrubby sea-blite can grow up to four feet tall, and its thickets form distinctive landmarks on, for instance, Blakeney Point, Norfolk, and Chesil Beach, Dorset. They are also landmarks for migrating small birds, which often use them as refuges.

Common bistort, *Persicaria bistorta* (VN: Dock; Easter ledges, Easter ledger; Easterman giants; Easter May-giants; Water ledges; Pudding grass, Pudding dock; Snake-weed; Pink pokers). Only botanists and southerners use the name 'bistort' for *Persicaria bistorta*. It is an awkward piece of anglicised Latin, probably meaning 'twice-twisted' and referring to the contorted root (hence 'snake-weed'). To those who live in its heartland, up in the north Pennines,

Common bistort. The leaves are used in a spring pudding in the north.

and especially in the fellside villages between Halifax and
Carlisle, it is known simply as 'dock' or 'pudding dock', or
occasionally by one of the other names that refer to its central role in a traditional springtime pudding made from the
cooked leaves and various combinations of oatmeal, egg and
other green herbs. Easter May-giants, Easterman giants (or
sometimes Easter mangiants) are derivations from the
French *manger*, to eat. (A nineteenth-century dictionary of
Cumbrian dialect has a wonderful phonetic rendering of the
name Easterman giants: 'Easter-mun-jiands (EE,STTHUR'R'-
MU'JAAI'NTS)'.)

*Common sorrel.
The leaves are
refreshingly sharp,
like young plum-
skins.*

Bistort was also once called 'passion dock', and the pudding almost certainly originated as a cleansing, bitter dish
for Lent, traditionally eaten in the two weeks before Easter.
It was an obvious choice for such a recipe. The dock grows
in dense patches in damp meadows and pastures, on river-
banks and roadsides, and occasionally in wet woodland
clearings. (One aficionado from the Calder Valley in West
Yorkshire swears the best crop came from his grandfather's
grave on Sowerby Top.) The long-stalked, heart-shaped
leaves are well developed by Easter, and are unmistakable
amongst the grass because of their ribbed tops and silvery
undersides, which flash in the March winds.

Varieties of dock pudding have been eaten on a local
basis in the north Pennines for centuries, but began to
attract national attention in 1971, when the 'World Champi-
onship Dock Pudding Contest' was inaugurated in the
Calder Valley, around the villages of Hebden Bridge and
Mytholmroyd. The competition, which is still kept up,
brought many memories and recipes to the surface: 'As kids
we used to go out with carrier bags and collect the first
sprouts of dock leaves. We would sell them to the house-
wives in the village, who would inspect the quality and give
us two shillings or half a crown depending on how good
they were.'[29]

The competitors are required to follow a basic recipe
including dock leaves, chopped nettles, onions, oatmeal and
seasoning, all fried in bacon fat. But dock pudding is a dish
for which every village, and maybe every family, has its own
recipe. Cumbria, still the dock-pudding centre, despite the
Calder Valley's higher profile, shows the range of local
flourishes and variations which can be added to this essen-

tially simple dish. The following recipe is from Raughton-head Women's Institute, just south of Carlisle: 'Take a small quantity of nettles, cabbage or young leaves and shoots from Brussels sprouts, kale or curly greens, three or four dandelions or [common] dock leaves, three good leeks and a good handful of the herb known in Cumberland as Easterman Giants, plus two or three gooseberry or blackcurrant leaves may be added. Cook in a little water and add some cooked barley. Chop and mix greens with barley. Serve as it is or with eggs or have an egg and oatmeal beaten in.'[30]

From Carlisle itself: 'We used to gather dandelion leaves, young ones, and nettles, also young ones, Easter ledges from the churchyard, all chopped up with two new sticks of rhubarb, bound with beaten egg and pearl barley, put in a cloth and boiled.'[31]

And from Beetham, down below Kendal: 'The leaves are washed and chopped up like mint and mixed with a dumpling mixture, either vegetable or suet, rolled and chopped into slices and fried with bacon fat. Serve with a grilled dish.'[32]

A more sophisticated Cumbrian recipe, involving rolling and skewering the leaves and then simmering them in milk and butter, was noted by a visitor from Epping Forest in Essex.[33] In fact, Epping, and the river valleys and wet commons surrounding it, are one of the southern strongholds of the species, so perhaps the emergence of Essex dock kebab is not an impossibility.

Common sorrel, *Rumex acetosa* (VN: Sour docks, Sour dogs, Sour dots, Sour ducks, Sour grabs, Sour sabs, Sour sap, Sour sops, Soorocks; Vinegar plant, Vinegar leaves; Rain; Green sauce, Bread and sauce; Sugar stick – stems only). Sorrel's reputation as a sour-tasting plant is echoed in almost every one of its common names. Yet sour isn't really the right description at all, suggesting something as painfully, tartly dry as a sloe. Sorrel leaves are more like the skins of young plums, sharp, astringent and refreshing. Nearly two centuries ago John Clare described how parched field-workers would chew them raw to slake their thirst.[34]

Sorrel leaves are still nibbled by children across Britain, and increasingly used in salads, soups and sauces for fish. A woman from the Baltic serves sorrel soup with hard-boiled egg, just as spinach soup is served in eastern Europe.[35] But the taste of cooked sorrel is closer to rhubarb than spinach. A fascinating recipe from the 1930s exploits this fruitiness by using the leaves in a turnover: 'In Lancashire they still use the fresh young leaves of wild sorrel as a substitute for apple in turnovers. I have made it myself, and very good it is, with plenty of brown sugar and a little moisture on the leaves. Sorrel is in season between apple and gooseberries, i.e. in April and May.'[36]

Garlic mustard, whose leaves are a good addition to spring salads.

Sorrel is still common on road-verges and river-banks and in grassland of all kinds (except 'improved', reseeded meadowland). Where it grows in quantity, its flower-spikes

float like a red haze amongst the grasses in May and June. The leaves are arrow-shaped and grow both from the stem and at the base of the plant. In seashore sites, they can become almost succulent.

Garlic mustard or **Jack-by-the-hedge**, *Alliaria petiolata*, is an abundant herb of hedge-banks and woods, smelling mildly of garlic. It has long been used as a flavouring: in sauces for fish and lamb in the seventeenth and eighteenth centuries, and as an ingredient for spring salads today.[37] In 1993 it was being sold for a pound a bunch in a smart Italian delicatessen in London's Covent Garden.[38] Jack-by-the-hedge is a biennial, and the soft, nettle-shaped leaves can be picked from September, when they first begin to show, until late spring, when the brilliant white flowers appear.

Water-cress, *Rorippa nasturtium-aquaticum*, is the only British native plant which has passed into large-scale commercial cultivation scarcely altered from its wild state (or perhaps I should say 'states': there are 10 other closely related species and hybrids, of which three are the chief ones used in commerce).

Water-cress was traditionally picked wild from the edges of fast-flowing streams, where it can grow in thick drifts. It was important enough for settlements to be named after it – e.g. Kersey, Suffolk ('cress island'); Kesgrave, also in Suffolk ('ditch or grove where cress grew'); Kersal, Lancashire ('the haugh [flat alluvial land] where cress grew'); and Kershope, Cumbria ('cress valley').[39] But John Evelyn, in *Acetaria: A Discourse of Sallets*, refers to it rather disparagingly as 'the vulgar *Water-Cress*', one of two salad vegetables which are 'best for raw and cold Stomacks, but nourish little'.[40] It became more fashionable in the eighteenth century, when its anti-scorbutic properties were realised, and by the nineteenth century it was certainly under small-scale cultivation, especially in areas where there were clear chalk streams, such as Wiltshire and the north Chilterns. Henry Mayhew made a fascinating first-hand record of the water-cress trade in Victorian London:

'The first coster-cry heard of a morning in the London streets is of "Fresh wo-orter-creases". Those that sell them have to be on their rounds in time for the mechanics' breakfast, or the day's gains are lost … At the principal

Water-cress, common in shallow streams and best used cooked, in soups, for instance.

entrance to Farringdon market there is an open space, running the entire length of the railings in front and extending from the iron gates at the entrance to the sheds down the centre of the large paved court before the shops. In this open space the cresses are sold, by the salesmen or saleswomen to whom they are consigned, in the hampers they are brought in from the country ... The market – by the time we reach it – has just begun; one dealer has taken his seat, and sits motionless with cold – for it wants but a month to Christmas – with his hands thrust deep into the pockets of his grey driving coat. Before him is an opened hamper with a candle fixed in the centre of the bright green cresses, and as it shines through the wicker sides of the basket, it casts curious patterns on the ground – as a night shade does.'[41]

Special railway tracks – 'Watercress lines' – were established to run the crop up to London and are still referred to by this name in north Hampshire and near Stamford in Lincolnshire.[42]

Water-cress grown commercially in beds has the advantage over the wild form of growing in water drawn directly from underground springs or bore-holes and isolated from the surrounding land by concrete or chalk channels. It thus avoids the danger – always, unfortunately, a threat with wild cresses – of picking up larvae of the fluke, *Fasciola hepatica*, which attacks and severely damages the livers of sheep and cattle, and can do the same to humans. The fluke is transmitted through a complicated cycle involving a pond snail. The larvae hatch from eggs in the sheep's droppings and 'swim' through the damp grass until they reach an area of water where the snails live. They burrow into the snails' soft tissues, multiply and metamorphose, before escaping and swimming to the water's edge. Here they crawl onto vegetation, including water-cress, and wait for the plant to be eaten by grazing animals (or foraging humans, for that matter) so that the whole cycle can begin again.

One picker, to be on the safe side, follows the same rule as is applied to shellfish: 'Water-cress growing wild should never be eaten when there is an "r" in the month'[43] – though I am afraid this is a rather contracted view of the fluke's ingenious breeding cycle. The only way to ensure you are eating fluke-free cresses is to pick plants growing *in* fast-flowing, clean water (preferably over chalk) and not from the banks; and, to be doubly sure, turn them into soups: cooking kills all stages of the fluke.

This is not to say that cultivated cresses are utterly without hazards. Although they are unmistakable when in flower, with four-petalled white flowers on top of the swaying hummocks of green, at other times they can be mistaken for a few other species with similar leaves that cohabit with them in running chalk-rich water. I have twice found sprigs of fool's water-cress (*Apium nodiflorum*) – not very pleasant eating, but fortunately not poisonous – tangled up with bunches of supermarket water-cress.

An up-and-coming cousin of water-cress is **Walthamstow yellow-cress**, *R.* × *armoracioides*, a speciality of the damp wasteland round Walthamstow Reservoirs in north London. It is a hybrid between **creeping yellow-cress**, *R. sylvestris*, and **Austrian yellow-cress**, *R. austriaca*, an introduced species whose nearest locality is some miles from Walthamstow. Just how it got together with its cousin is still a mystery.

Horse-radish, *Armoracia rusticana*, is a common perennial of waste ground and roadsides in England, though very scarce in Scotland. No one is sure when it arrived in this country from its native western Asia, but it was certainly well before 1548. That year William Turner remarked that it 'groweth in Morpeth in Northumberland and there it is called Redco'. Fifty years later, Gerard was recommending it as being preferable to mustard as a condiment for meat.[44] Even then, its deep, spreading tap-roots must have been building up large and tenacious colonies in untended ground – a process which can be seen most strikingly today in the extensive troops on railway embankments.

Horse-radish does not produce its sprays of white flowers every year in this country. But its long, crinkled leaves are unmistakable, and smell slightly of horse-radish root if crushed between the fingers. Digging up the roots of wild plants is illegal on private land except where you have the landowner's permission. But horse-radish is frequent enough in the rough corners of gardens and allotments for some to be likely to be within legal access. In the Fens it was regarded as a gleaner's perk when farmland was being ploughed: 'Horseradish grew on the roadsides. Men came on bikes with sacks and dug it to sell. When Grassfield was ploughed, Jimmy Greenwood (a well-known hawker) followed the plough and picked up horseradish to sell it.'[45]

The labour of excavating and extracting its intricate, woody and pungent roots is followed by the ordeal of peel-

Horse-radish, introduced from Asia by the sixteenth century, is now common on roadsides.

ing and grating them. This can end in tears worse than result from the most blinding onions: 'A Russian friend suggested to us that we should deep-freeze the root first and then grate it after peeling. In this way the effect on the eyes can be avoided.'[46]

There are all manner of recipes for turning the grated root into sauces and condiments, but none to match the formula of the flamboyant and reforming nineteenth-century chef Alexis Soyer (author of *Shilling Cookery for the People*). It is called, with some justification, 'The Universal Devil's Mixture':

'Put in a bowl a good tablespoonful of Durham mustard ... mix with four tablespoonfuls of Chilli vinegar. Add to it a tablespoonful of grated horseradish, two bruised shallots, a teaspoonful of salt, half ditto of Cayenne, ditto of black pepper, and one of pounded sugar, two teaspoonfuls of chopped chillies, if handy. Add the yolks of two raw eggs. Take a paste brush, and after having slightly seasoned each piece [of meat] with salt, rub over each piece with the same, probing some into the incisions. First broil slowly and then the last few minutes as near as possible to the Pandemonium fire.'[47]

Dittander, *Lepidium latifolium*, is a tall perennial native of damp ground near the sea on the east and south coasts, and introduced or naturalised in a few places inland, for instance by the Grand Union Canal in London, and along a considerable stretch of the main road east out of Baldock, Hertfordshire, where it has been since at least 1929.[48] In flower dittander resembles a small-leaved horse-radish, and its roots have a similar hot and pungent taste. Before the introduced horse-radish (see above) became fashionable, dittander was picked, and occasionally cultivated, for use as a condiment.

It was also once a standard herbal treatment for leprous sores, and in 1990 a Sussex botanist found a colony growing on ground once occupied by Chichester's oldest hospital – the Hospital of St James and Mary Magdalen, which was established in the twelfth century (safely outside the medieval city walls) specifically to care for lepers.[49] This discovery prompted John Palmer, from north Kent, to notice that the only three established colonies of dittander that he had found in this part of the county were *all* close to the sites of turn-of-the-century hospitals: Bexley Hospital, near Dartford Heath (opened in 1898); Joyce Green Hospital, on Dartford Marshes (opened 1902); and the Old G.L.C. Southern Hospital at Darenth (opened 1890 but now demolished).[50] It stretches credibility that dittander was still being cultivated as a leprosy herb at the end of the nineteenth century, but so does the possibility that all three sites are near hospitals purely by coincidence.

Sea-kale, *Crambe maritima*, is one of the largest and most striking of all maritime plants, and in the few places where it occurs in quantity – now very few, sadly – it dominates the shorescape. From a distance the tightly clumped plants look like enormous sea-urchins, or a rotund desert cactus that has taken to the shingle. Closer to, they have something of the character of outsize cauliflowers. The domed sprays of white flowers are held above, and partly wrapped by, fleshy, glaucous blue-green leaves, which at the base of the plant can be 12 to 18 inches long. The single, small colony that survives on the north Norfolk coast at Cley (deliberately planted there in 1912)[51] is a well-known landmark on the walk out to Blakeney Point.

Children in Anglesey have had ingenious fun with the outsize leaves and round green seeds: 'In Cemlyn Bay [they] used it when playing shop – the leaves representing cabbage and the fruit, peas.'[52]

But sea-kale's main attraction has always been as a vegetable delicacy. For centuries, on south-coast beaches and cliffs, coastal dwellers would cut the young shoots, especially where they had been naturally blanched while growing up through the shingle or sand. In some places, locals would watch for the shoots to appear in the early spring and heap seaweed or sand over them to make the blanched shoots extend even further. At Dungeness in Kent (which still has one of the biggest colonies in Britain) this custom continued into living memory: 'Many years before the nuclear power station I can remember locals kicking shingle over the plants in early spring to blanch the shoots.'[53]

To judge from contemporary records sea-kale was abundant along the south coast in the eighteenth century. There was some trade in the shoots at local markets, and it was grown by a few specialist gardening enthusiasts. Gilbert White sowed some in his garden at Selborne on 6 April

Sea-kale, on the shingle at Cemlyn Bay, Anglesey.

1751, with seed gathered on a visit to Devon the previous August.[54] But its status began to change when White's near neighbour, the distinguished Hampshire botanist William Curtis, popularised the vegetable with his pamphlet *Directions for the Culture of the Crambe Maritima or Sea Kale, for the Use of the Table* in 1799. As a result the plant was taken up by London society, and the demand at Covent Garden increased enormously. Fresh shoots – and, for that matter, roots and seeds – were now gathered for export, not just for home use.

The impact on some populations did not seem to be immediate. On the Isle of Man at the end of the nineteenth century, it was collected from the shore in cartloads: 'It was fashionable to collect the winter roots for forcing, and junior civil servants had to affect pleasure when their seniors made them presents of the fresh shoots.'[55]

The feathery leaves and gherkin-like seed-cases of sweet cicely are pleasantly aniseed-flavoured.

According to Devon naturalists, it was still 'very frequent' in the county in 1915. But by 1939, the Revd Keble Martin, editor of the great *Flora of Devon*, described it as 'much less common than it used to be', and blamed erosion of the cliffs as well as the gathering of the roots for cultivation.

That is a fair statement of the sea-kale's contemporary status; and it is probable that its slow decline is due now more to the instability and human disturbance of many coastal habitats than to uprooting.

Salad burnet, *Sanguisorba minor*, is a short herb of chalk and limestone grassland throughout Britain, sometimes abundant enough for the leaflets to scent the air with cucumber when you walk over them. They are slightly bitter to the taste, but have long been used as a salad green,[56] and as a cooling addition to summer drinks.

The round, rust-speckled flower-heads, a little like scabs or blood clots, made it a signaturist's favourite, for staunching wounds – hence the Latin name '*sanguisorba*'. But for one budding eighteenth-century botanist – the Revd Gilbert White – it was burnet's more palpable strengths that made the deepest impression. On 6 July 1765, he was riding back to his brother's house across the Hampshire hills and was struck by how, despite the privations of a long drought, the downs were still kept green by this diminutive plant: 'The downs between Alresford & Andover are full of

Burnet: so full in many places that it is almost the only herb that covers the Ground: & is eaten down very close by the sheep, who are fond of it ... It is worth observation that this herb seems to abound most in the poorest, & shallowest chalkey soil ... Near Waller's Ash I rode thro a piece of Ground of about 400 acres, which had been lately pared by a breast plough for burning: here the burnet was coming-up very quick on the bare ground, tho' the crown of the root must have been cut off of course along with the turf: this shews that it is a plant tenacious of life, since it springs from the severed root like plantain.'[57]

Sweet cicely, *Myrrhis odorata* (VN: The Myrrh, Liquorice plant). Although it is probably an ancient introduction to Britain, sweet cicely looks thoroughly at home by rivers and lanes in the north – especially where its extravagantly

feathery leaf-sprays and pure white flowers are standing against a drystone wall. All parts of the plant taste and smell pleasantly of aniseed, though the adjective 'sweet' may also apply to a sugary undertone in the taste. John Gerard enjoyed the roots, boiled like parsnips, and the leaves were sometimes added to stewed fruit dishes to reduce the amount of sugar needed. But today, it is the long seed-cases which are most frequently used. They have something of the appearance of small gherkins whilst they are still green in June and have become a popular wayside nibble and unusual salad ingredient.[58] A wood-turner in Middlesbrough regularly uses the oily seed-cases to polish his finished pieces (which echoes the old Westmorland practice of using the leaves to polish oak panels).[59]

Alexanders, naturalised in St George's churchyard, Isle of Portland.

Like other species of uncertain origin, myths have gathered around sweet cicely's provenance. One contributor from the Welsh borders believes that its distribution in some places may reflect ancient historical boundaries: 'On the roadside verges around Selattyn, sweet cicely grows in such profusion that it has completely taken over from the other common umbellifers as the dominant hedgerow plant; yet south and east of Oswestry – and over Offa's Dyke – it becomes a rare plant. I cannot think that weather, soil or climate can change so greatly in three miles as to cause this difference, and wonder if this is a cultural boundary rather than a physical one, perhaps between Celtic use of the plant against the plague, not held by, or passed on to, the invading Saxons beyond the Dyke.'[60]

In the Isle of Man sweet cicely is believed to bloom on Old Christmas Eve, and there has been a small revival of a custom of searching for blooms on this day:
'The Myrrh, as it is known here, was used as a proof that the new calendar was not to be trusted. It was looked on to flower on Old Christmas Eve, 5th January, and was often recorded as being brought into church on that day, in flower. It was as often said that it was not truly in flower by the embarrassed minister, and it was only a very new leaf that was unfurling. However I have seen, on a number of occasions, that after a mild winter it is indeed possible for a small bud to develop this early ... The Myrrh is often found near the doors of old houses. There are many clumps of it at Cregneash, the Manx Museum. Within the

last ten years a local newspaper showed a photograph of it in flower at Old Christmas.'[61]

Alexanders, *Smyrnium olustratum.* The glossy green leaves of alexanders are often the first new foliage of the year to appear on hedge-banks close to the sea. It was originally a Mediterranean plant, the 'parsley of Alexandria', and was probably first introduced to this country by the Romans as an all-purpose spring vegetable and tonic. Almost every part of the plant was used, from the root to the young flower-buds, which were pickled like miniature cauliflowers. It was cultivated in monastic herb gardens in the medieval period, which perhaps explains the colonies often found on the sites of old religious foundations, for instance on Steepholm in the Bristol Channel, where there was an Augustinian community in the twelfth century, and at an unusual inland site in Bedfordshire: 'At Elstow the plants occur not far from the Abbey Church and the remains of the former Benedictine Abbey, founded around 1078, which suggests that Alexanders was first grown in this area in the Abbey gardens as a vegetable for the nuns, prior to the Act of Dissolution in 1539.'[62] It also sometimes occurs near castles.

It continued to be cultivated in cottage gardens until the early eighteenth century, when it was supplanted by celery. By then it was becoming well naturalised, with a clear preference for sites close to the sea, where large colonies of bushy plants up to four feet high can develop. (Though it does occur sporadically inland. I have seen it, for instance, near villages on the eastern edge of Dartmoor.)

Alexanders has a pungent, angelica-like savour that is probably too pronounced for it to make a comeback as a vegetable. But it is worth trying the thicker stems, where they have been blanched by the plant's own leaf-sheaths, cooked like celery.

Pignut, *Conopodium majus* (VN: Ground nut, Cat nut, Earth nut, Earth chestnut, Yennett, Jog-journals). Digging for the dark-brown tubers of pignut used to be a common habit amongst country children. The nuts are usually between six and eight inches under the earth, and, eaten raw, their white flesh has something of the crisp taste of young hazel-nuts: 'Between the wars my uncle, an ex-sailor, would take me walking through the fields of the West Riding. He

Pignut, once harvested for its edible nut-like tubers which have the flavour of parsnips or young hazel-nuts.

Fennel, probably introduced by the Romans as a herb for digestive problems, now widely naturalised, especially near the coast.

would regularly stop everything to plunge his knife into the ground and dig up a "pig nut" about the size of a walnut or chestnut, peel it and offer it to me to eat. He deplored the poor supply, saying that 40 years previously you could dig up enough to feed four people in a half an hour. These would be cooked in a "Dutch Oven" with rabbit joints. Pignuts cooked have the texture of and a milder taste than parsnips.'[63]

If they are less common now, it is a result not of over-zealous foragers, but of loss of habitat. Pignut, a modest-sized umbellifer with fine, thready foliage, is a plant of long-established grassland and open woodland, except on chalk, and has declined just as these places have. It is, sadly, probably fortunate that digging for the tubers is now illegal except where the landowner has given permission.

Fennel, *Foeniculum vulgare*. For all its aggressive growth in some places, fennel never looks convincingly native on British waysides. Its hair-like plumes of bright green leaves seem foppish and exotic by the side of rustic native relatives such as hogweed. In fact, it was probably introduced by the Romans as a medicinal and culinary herb. It is now widely naturalised across Britain, especially near the sea, where it grows on roadsides, sand-dunes and sea-walls. Inland it is a plant more of waste ground and tips, originating often from discarded seeds.

The leaves smell strongly of aniseed, and are widely used in cooking, especially with oily fish. A sauce of chopped fennel and gooseberry is a classic accompaniment to mackerel. The seeds can also be used as a cooking herb, or as an after-dinner *digestif* (they are often served at the end of a meal in Indian restaurants). This practice has a history going back at least to the Middle Ages: 'In Fennel-seed, this vertue you shall finde,/ Foorth of your lower parts to drive the winde'.[64]

In Gwent, children make pens out of the hard stalks.[65]

Wild marjoram, *Origanum vulgare*. This is the same species as the 'oregano' that is such a characteristic herb of Mediterranean cooking. It does not develop quite such an earthy fragrance in our cooler climate, but it is still an ex-cellent herb in the kitchen and common enough in rough calcareous grassland throughout Britain for small-scale gathering of sprigs and leaves to be acceptable. It is a peren-

Wild thyme on river-bank shingle.

nial, growing up to two feet tall, with purple, pink or sometimes white flowers in bunches at the top of the stems, and
attracting many species of butterfly in high summer.

   Thyme, *Thymus vulgaris*. This is the thyme normally
used in cooking, a Mediterranean species which sometimes
persists as a garden throw-out on old walls and dry banks.
There are three other species native to Britain: **Breckland
thyme**, *T. serpyllum*, confined to sandy heaths in west Suffolk and Norfolk; **large thyme**, *T. pulegioides*, a sprawling,
larger-leaved species, locally frequent in short chalky or
sandy grassland in southern and central England; and **wild
thyme**, *T. polytrichus*. This last is by far the most widespread and abundant species. It is confined to the chalk in
south-east England, but elsewhere will grow on acid, short-

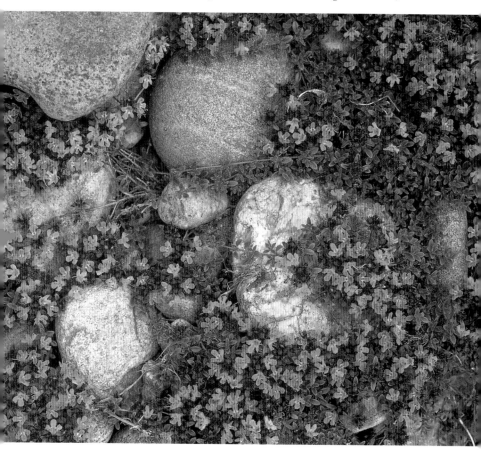

turfed pastures, ant-hills in meadows, cliffs, walls and rocky places. Wild thyme often grows in large mats, especially on the chalk, and provides one of the memorable scents of walks over the southern downlands in warm sunshine. Both our common wild species are fragrant enough to be serviceable in cooking.

All species of thyme contain the characteristic volatile oil, thymol, which is a reasonably powerful antiseptic. Perhaps it was some inkling of this quality which led to the herb being a key ingredient in Judges' posies and the Sovereign's Maundy Thursday posy, which were both devices originally intended to afford the carriers some protection from the infectious diseases of the poor.

'In the Western Isles wild thyme, which grows abundantly, was put under the pillow or drunk as an infusion to prevent nightmares or otherwise give a restful sleep. Thyme tea was popular throughout the Highlands as an everyday beverage. In an area where lavender would not grow well, women used flowering sprigs of thyme to scent their clothes, handkerchiefs and household linen.'[66]

Other fragrant Mediterranean herbs sometimes become naturalised on old walls and dry ground, for instance **winter savory**, *Satureja montana*, at Beaulieu Abbey, Hampshire; **rosemary**, *Rosmarinus officinalis*, especially in graveyards, where it is planted as a symbol of remembrance; and **lavender**, usually *Lavandula × intermedia*, a hybrid of *L. angustifolia*. Self-sown lavender seedlings are increasingly common both in and outside gardens in southern England – perhaps an indication of the trend towards milder winters.

Mints. There are some 14 or 15 mint species and hybrids found growing wild or naturalised in Britain. Some are escaped garden cultivars, such as **apple mint**, *Mentha × villosa*; others are natives which have been taken into cultivation. Most grow in damp places: woodland clearings, pondsides, humus-rich waste ground, and all have the characteristic mint-scent – though there are many variations on this. In 1798, William Sole published a survey of British mints (he included 25 separate kinds), and his vivid attempts to pin down their different scents is the most entertaining feature of the book.[67] **Corn mint**, *M. arvensis*, 'has a strong fullsome mixed smell of mellow apples and gingerbread' –

which is certainly more complimentary than Grigson's 'wet, mouldy gorgonzola'. (Sole's spotting of the hint of gingerbread was perceptive, and corn mint is almost certainly the ancestor of the yellow-striped garden variety known as 'ginger mint'.) His 'strong-scented mint' – which may be our **sharp-toothed mint**, *M.* × *villosonervata* – 'has a very strong volatile mixed smell of volatile salt and amber, camphor, and mint' and is 'an honourable relic of our venerable Gothick ruins'. The scent of **water mint**, *M. aquatica*, 'is exactly that of a ropy chimney in a wet summer, where wood fires have been kept in winter-time'. (Water mint, incidentally, has a bronze-leaved variety which seems to be confined to pond-edges and damp flushes on limestone and which possesses a distinct Eau-de-Cologne scent, though true Eau-de-Cologne mint is usually referred to var. *citrata* of peppermint.)

Peppermint, *M.* × *piperita*, is the most commercially exploited species, for its essential oil which is used both in medicine and in cooking. A Surrey woman remembers gathering it (and many other medicinal herbs) during the Second World War:
'At the beginning of the war, through writing to a newspaper, I was put in touch with Messrs Brome and Schimmer, druggists in London, who supplied hospitals. Mr Brome came down to see me to make sure I knew the plants, because in the First War some enthusiastic gatherers had mixed poisonous and non-poisonous plants ... In our spare time we gathered and dried the plants and sent them off by train in sacks. We didn't get great quantities. The dried weight is so little compared with the gathered plant, but the druggists were very pleased with the quality of what we sent and the money they gave us we gave to the Red Cross. Among the plants we gathered were foxglove leaves (for the heart), nettles, coltsfoot leaves (for asthma), wood betony and agrimony (tonics) and peppermint for flavouring. Our room at home had strings stretched across between the picture rails hung with bunches of drying herbs. When we had peppermint drying my mother and I went to sleep in our chairs.'[68]

Woodruff, *Galium odoratum*. 'Woodruff' was 'woodrove' in the sixteenth century, and it may have been a plant that 'roved', or spread, through woods. But the name is

*Woodruff growing
around – and on –
a dead elm stump.*

more likely to be a simple, literal description. There are no more perfectly formed woodland plants in early May, with their tiny, chalk-white flowers on upright stems decked out with bright green six-leaved ruffs.

Whilst they are growing the plants are almost odourless. But, picked and dried, they quickly develop the fresh smell of new-mown hay, which later takes on hints of almond. The leaves will retain this scent for many months, and woodruff – traditionally called 'sweet woodruff' – was once held in high regard as an all-purpose domestic freshener. Dried bunches were hung in wardrobes to deter moths and laid amongst stored linen. The leaf-whorls were used as bookmarks, and 'during Georgian times they were placed in the cases of pocket-watches, so that their fragrance could be inhaled whenever telling the time'.[69] They also found their way into snuffs, pot-pourris, pillows, and 'sweet waters' for improving the complexion.

The scent is taken up quickly by liquids. I was taught to steep dried woodruff in apple juice by an Austrian living in the Chilterns (where the plant is abundant in the beech-woods). And it is in Austria and Germany, especially along the banks of the Rhine, that it forms a key ingredient of 'Maibowl', a punch which is drunk on 1 May, and which is made by steeping a bunch of dried woodruff in Moselle or Rhine wine flavoured with sliced orange and sugar.

Woodruff occurs throughout the British Isles, but in East Anglia it is scarce and virtually confined to ancient woodland. In central and southern England, it has a prefer-ence for old woodland and hedge-banks on chalky soils. In the west and the north it is more tolerant and can be found in shady places of all kinds, including hollow lanes and stream-banks.

It no longer grows in London, but was once hung in churches in the City (as elsewhere) on St Barnabas Day, 11 June. A small turning off Tower Hill, now Cooper's Row, was once called Woodruff Lane, a name commemorated in a tablet on the wall.[70]

Dandelion, *Taraxacum* species (VN: Jack-piss-the-bed, Pissy beds, Pittley beds, Tiddle-beds, Wet-the-bed; Dog's posy, Old man's clock, Peasant's clock, Swine's snout; seeds: Fairies, Parachutes, Sugar eaters).

Dandelions mean carpets of golden-yellow flowers,

jagged green leaves (the *dent de lion* – 'lion's tooth') and clouds of featherweight seeds blowing in the wind. Albrecht Dürer saw the appeal even of the closed and withering flower-heads and included them in his extraordinary close-up portrait (painted in 1503) of a square foot of meadow-land, *Large Tuft of Herbs*. Shakespeare understood the popular familiarity with the whole plant, as well as local Midlands names for it,[71] and included them in the elegy in

Cymbeline: 'Golden lads and girls all must/ As chimney-sweepers come to dust.' Keats imagined 'The soft rustle of a maiden's gown/ Fanning away the dandelion's down'.[72]

Children still blow dandelion down from the round dandelion clocks – the 'chimney-sweepers' – to 'tell the time'. The number of blows needed to remove all the seeds gives the hour. If you can catch one on the wing, you can make a wish.[73] Other children's games with dandelions robustly ignore the myth passed down in some families that even touching the plant will make you wet your bed:

'Take a long stalk of dandelion, remove the head, and split one end downwards approximately half an inch. Place the split inside your mouth and blow gently. A raspberry sound should be made.'[74]

'We made bracelets of dandelion stems, tucking the narrow end into the wide end.'[75]

'We used the white latex from the stem to draw on pavements.'[76]

But dandelion is still widely known as wet-the-bed or pissy bed by children across Britain, and it has long been used as a herbal diuretic and laxative. Its reputation has been confirmed scientifically in a number of studies (e.g. at the North London Polytechnic in 1978), and as a bonus it contains high levels of potassium, an element which is removed from the body when urine production is stepped up. A Cambridgeshire man whose family have been seed-merchants since the 1890s recalls the high repute in which dandelion's medicinal powers have been held in this country: 'In the 1920s, when times were very bad for this district, it was quite usual for families to go out and dig up dandelion roots in the fields, the wild ones, and sell them to the chemist to buy bread. But also, particularly in the 1880s, it was customary for the gentry to grow dandelions in their unheated greenhouses for winter salads. As you know, they are very beneficial for flushing out the kidneys and helped to prevent the rich port-drinking inhabitants from getting gout. Dandelion salads were very popular in those days; also sandwiches of thin brown bread and butter filled with dandelion leaves were served by the ladies for afternoon tea.

My father was very friendly with the well-known Snell family who ran the famous Royal Nurseries in Broad

Albrecht Dürer's watercolour 'Large Tuft of Herbs' (1503), which clearly shows dandelion, as well as yarrow and greater plantain leaves.

Street, Ely [now defunct]. Gradually we took over the postal distribution of dandelion seed but at first it was locally grown … One point worth making is that in the 1880s it was difficult to grow lettuce throughout the winter months. Today it is easy with the modern varieties. But of course dandelion has a very distinctive flavour and it seems to be growing in popularity. We sell more seed each year. This may be a reaction against the modern greenhouse-produced, rather tasteless lettuce.'[77]

Certainly dandelions are now much more familiar to British cooks. The traditional French dish *pissenlit au lard*, fried bacon scraps and croutons served on a dandelion salad, is found increasingly on menus, and I have noticed dandelion leaves in ordinary pub salads. New treatments and recipes – for dandelion pasta, pickled dandelions, dandelion

Left: Andy Goldsworthy's spring stamp design, made entirely from dandelion heads.

and mozzarella pie (see p. 13) and stir-fried dandelion – are being developed all the time: 'I couldn't come to terms with any of the dandelion family; the bitterness was just too unbearable to my taste. I tried, before passing final sentence, lightly frying the leaves of dandelion and ratstail plantain in a little fat for a minute or two, and the result was exquisite. It turned the tough leaves into wafer-thin crisps, the bitterness into a gentle edge, and brought out the flavour which had always been masked by the bitterness.'[78]

The flowers can be added to dandelion salads and provide a welcome dash of colour and a soft, honey-flavoured foil to the leaves' tartness. But they are most usually gathered for making dandelion wine, the classic account of which is in Laurie Lee's *Cider with Rosie*. The roots provide a coffee substitute when roasted and ground, and they were much used during the Second World War when real coffee was unobtainable. Even the seeds are eaten – at least by cage-birds: 'A bird fancier of my acquaintance encourages dandelions in one corner of his allotment. He singes the down off the clocks with his cigarette lighter and feeds the seeds to his finches.'[79]

More than 200 microspecies of dandelion have been recognised in Britain, and all can be used in similar ways.

There are also large numbers of yellow-flowered hawk-bits, hawkweeds and hawk's-beards, etc, some of whose leaves are quite palatable but which have never been differentiated much (or used) at a popular level.

'Golden lads and girls all must/ As chimney-sweepers come to dust.' (Shakespeare)

Fruits

A few of the many species of wild fruit that grow
in Britain – for example, the crab-apple – have
cultivated descendants readily available in garden and
shop. But the majority are still found only in the
wild, with their zests and savours undiluted.
Bilberries are still widely harvested in the Welsh
borders and find their way into pub desserts.

Sloes are gathered for sloe gin – bottled at Michaelmas and drunk at Christmas. Blackberries have been taken into gardens, but the handful of cultivars cannot match the variety of the 400-odd subspecies, which all differ slightly in taste and texture.

Windfall wilding apples, often still edible deep into winter.

Juniper, *Juniperus communis*, provides the essential flavouring for one of the country's favourite spirits, gin. But native juniper has probably not been used by British distillers since the last century, and the berries are now mostly imported from eastern Europe. Home-grown fruits, however, are increasingly used as a flavouring, especially with game: 'The local limestone hill, Arnside Knott [Lancashire], provides us with juniper berries to cook with venison. Used whole they give a bitter, crunchy bite to savouries.' [1]

Limestone hills are just one of the favoured places of this evergreen shrub, which tends to grow in colonies and have a striking impact on local landscapes. It is widespread over much of Britain, but eccentrically local, occurring only on comparatively well-lit and well-drained rocks and soils. And its two classic habitats could hardly be more different. In the north it prefers cold, rainy sites on acid soils, growing with heather and bilberry on moorland and as an understorey in the Highland birch and pine woods. In the south,

it is a species of hot, dry, calcium-rich soils and haunts the parched downlands of chalk country.

The form of individual bushes is also very varied. They can be low and prostrate at one extreme, and conical or cylindrical at the other, sometimes up to 17 feet in height. Bushes can also be bent and trimmed by wind and browsing, and change shape spontaneously with age, the older ones having a tendency to die out from the centre and collapse. (This is evident in one of the most long-standing populations in Britain, on the Taynish peninsula in Argyll, where there are almost no young bushes.) From a distance a large colony of juniper can look like a fantastic piece of topiary, a landscape of tapers and sprays, dark shelves and swells.

In some regions, juniper seems to thrive best in places where there have been cycles of change in land-use, where, for example, a period of grazing, which produces well-lit bare ground and short turf ideal for the germination of juniper seeds, is followed by a period of abandonment, which allows the seedlings to grow on ungrazed. In the Lake District and Northumberland, for instance, it is possible that juniper's survival is related historically to the alternations between pasturing and small-scale mining that characterised the rural economy here.[2] In Teesdale, Durham, it often grows around farms and on the boundaries between the enclosed land and the common grazing, where the effect of such changes would be most strongly felt.

The aromatic berries of juniper are used for flavouring gin.

Until the end of the last century, the juniper on the fells of Upper Teesdale was put to a variety of uses. Boughs were cut for firewood (which burns with a cedar-like fragrance) and for making the bases of haystacks. Even its insidious prickles were turned to advantage: 'Juniper was often used as a substitute for barbed wire by being placed on the tops of stone walls ... 120 years ago, the berries of juniper, or "junifer" as it was called, were collected by families who travelled from Weardale, who would grind the berries down to flavour bread and cakes.'[3] In England, juniper is distinctive enough to have places named after it. On the Surrey downs, for example, there are a Juniper Hill, Hall and Bottom.[4] Sometimes the name outlives the plant that inspired it. In north Oxfordshire there is a single large bush outside the

Fox pub at Juniper Hill, the village immortalised in Flora
Thompson's *Lark Rise to Candleford*.[5] It is a relic of what
was presumably a much larger colony on Cottisford Heath.
This is where, before the late eighteenth-century enclosures,
squatters built the settlement that was to become 'Candleford' hamlet.

In southern England, juniper occurs patchily in many
chalk areas, especially in Wiltshire, where small bushes can
sometimes be seen on road embankments. The largest pop-
ulation in England is inside the Ministry of Defence's
Chemical and Biological Defence Establishment at Porton
Down, Wiltshire. Here, in buffer-land barricaded by high-
security fencing, there are more than 14,000 juniper bushes,
growing amongst heather in a community that is known

from nowhere else on the southern chalk. As on the northern fells, though, the youngest bushes seem to date from a release from grazing pressure, in this case the rapid decline in rabbit numbers caused by the myxomatosis epidemic.[6]

The oil extracted from juniper has an ancient reputation as an abortifacient (which may have echoes in the Victorian belief in the effectiveness of gin for the same purpose). In Lothian, in the medieval period, giving birth 'under the savin tree' was a euphemism for a miscarriage or juniper-provoked abortion.[7] Until at least the mid-1980s juniper pills (still on the market in 1993) were being advertised as 'The Lady's Friend' in the small ads in ladies' journals.[8]

The name 'savin' does not seem to have survived in Britain, but in Herefordshire, where the species does not grow in the wild, some kind of juniper was known as 'the savage tree' and was used as a horse medicine (Grigson, interestingly, quotes the name 'horse saving' from Cumberland)[9]: 'It was crushed up and put in very small quantities in horse feed, and was said to "ginger them up".'[10]

It is possible that this was a cultivated variety of a European juniper, *J. sabina*, which is known as 'savin', and which yields oil of savarin, more potent – and toxic – than that from common juniper.

Bilberry, *Vaccinium myrtillus* (VN: Blaeberry, Whortleberry, Whinberry, Wimberry; for fruits: Whorts, Hurts, Urts). Bilberry-picking transports one more thoroughly to the role of hunter-gatherer than even blackberrying. The fruit is virtually unknown in cultivation – a source of constant bafflement to anyone who has sampled the dark, winy berries. (Commercial blueberries are a larger and less flavoursome American species: see below.) Bilberry's favoured habitats are in wild places, too, on acid heaths and moors in the northern and western uplands and as an understorey in Scottish pine-woods. And, because the shrub is low-growing and the berries often hidden under the leaves, much of the collecting must be done on hands and knees. In a BBC documentary in the mid-1970s, a group of volunteers were marooned on Exmoor as an experiment in survival. They spent much of their time browsing for bilberries on all fours, and an anthropologist, who was one of the party, remarked that they resembled nothing so much as a troop of foraging chimps.

Juniper wood, Little Langdale, Lake District, showing the variety of forms in which the shrub occurs.

But bilberry-picking has always been a great social and family occasion, with slightly differing customs in different parts of Britain. (And different names: the fruits are 'hurts' in Surrey, for instance, and 'whorts' in Somerset.)[11] Bilberries in Devon are picked mainly on Exmoor and Dartmoor and cooked in pies. Picking them used to be a local cottage industry with its own 'Whort Sunday' celebrations in August.[12]

'When I was living at Nether Stowey [Somerset] in the 1970s, whort picking had just ceased to be a commercial activity, giving a seasonal income to the villagers. However it had not long gone, and the locals always recommended the wearing of wellingtons whilst picking because of the danger of adders.'[13] (This may have been an example of the frequent practice by local pickers of exaggerating dangers, to deter 'outsiders'.)

Other threats, ancient and modern, have sadly curtailed picking in parts of the north-west, including the Isle of Man:

'Bilberries occupy a place in the Manx way of life beyond the simple attraction of flavour. A number of families reserve the first Sunday in August as the right day for gathering them without being aware that they are participating in a custom from much earlier times. Laa Luanya, Quarter Day, was formerly observed on 1st August by climbing a nearby hill and indulging in riotous games and lovemaking. There are many accounts of local clergy preaching against the practice, and as late as 1820 a preacher named Glick went up South Barrule in order to deter its observance. There is evidence from one of the last native speakers of Manx that there was still a handful of young people keeping up the custom in the early part of the present century. For a long time previously the activity had been disguised under the euphemistic excuses of "looking for a well", or "gathering bilberries". [Now] the accident at Chernobyl has deterred many people from picking them for fear of contamination. How long it will be before people's confidence returns remains to be seen.'[14]

The heart of mass bilberry-picking is the Welsh border country:

'Considerable numbers of people still pick whinberries, some of them [in Condover, Shropshire] using the tradi-

Bilberries, once an important wild harvest in upland Britain.

tional coarse-toothed metal comb [known as a *peigne* in France] with which the berries can be relatively quickly stripped from the plants.'[15]

'Bilberries are always known as "wimberries" locally, and there is an almost ritual annual return to traditional picking places. They were very important as a crop up till the Second War. Picking wimberries by whole families (taking the kettle up to make tea) on the Stiperstones and Long Mynd and selling them to dealers to be sent away (for dye, mainly) would keep children in boots for the next winter. There are school log-book references over the whole area for days taken off for wimberry picking.'[16]

In Gwent: 'The most worthwhile crop is the bilberry, in these parts known as wimberries. Although they grow all over the mountains, there are only a few favoured areas on north-facing slopes where they grow in such numbers that they can be picked commercially. Around here this is a traditional summer job which in the past was an important help to the family finances. One lady told me that when she was a child she and her brothers and sisters had to pick enough wimberries to buy their winter shoes. Today, most people pick enough just for their freezers, but a few dedicated pickers pick for the market and supply local shops, or sell to others for their freezers.'[17]

Wimberry tarts and pies are sold in pubs around Shrop-shire and the Marches. In Yorkshire they are known as 'mucky-mouth' pies and served as part of funeral teas. In a hotel in Hawes, North Yorkshire, I have eaten a traditional bilberry dessert, with the fruits (flavoured with a few sprigs of mint) baked in a Yorkshire pudding.

Hybrid bilberry, *V. vitis-idaea* × *V. myrtillus*, a cross between the bilberry and its just-about-edible cousin the cowberry (*V. vitis-idaea*), was first discovered on the Maer Hills in North Staffordshire in 1870. It also grows now on Cannock Chase. It is fertile and sets edible fruits.[18] **Blue-berry**, *V. corymbosum*, the larger-fruited American bilberry, now grown commercially in many parts of Britain, is natu-

Cranberry 'hummocks' on Abbots Moss, Cheshire. The closely related American species is used for cranberry sauce.

ralised from bird-sown seed on heathland in south Hampshire and Dorset. **Cranberry**, *V. oxycoccos*, is a low shrub of bogs and very wet heaths, with bright pink flowers, but not always producing the round to pear-shaped, edible orange-red fruits. Those used in cranberry sauce are usually from the **American cranberry**, *V. macrocarpon*, which is grown on a small scale commercially in Britain and naturalised in a few peaty places. **Bearberry**, *Arctostaphylos uva-ursi*, is a locally common shrub in rocky moorland in northern Britain. The shiny red berries are sharp but edible – as are the black fruits of the rarer **mountain bearberry**, *A. alpina*.

Gooseberry, *Ribes uva-crispa* (VN: Goosegogs). A spiny bush, with small hairy berries, gooseberry occurs through-

Right: gooseberries painted by Sir William Hooker, one of the foremost botanical illustrators of the nineteenth century.

out Britain – in deciduous woodland (where it often fails to fruit), hedges, scrub and occasionally rooted in drystone walls. The fruit appears in late May and is usually ripe enough to eat by mid-July (though it is rather sharp and dry without cooking). A wild bush with wine-coloured berries was found by a contributor in Banffshire.[19]

This humble wild fruit was the ancestor of all domestic gooseberries, including the most sumptuous dessert varieties, and the story of its transformation is a remarkable example of grass-roots plant-breeding. There is no record in Britain of the introduction of any cultivated varieties, nor of cultivation itself beginning before the sixteenth century. English gardeners domesticated the plant by taking in promising specimens from the wild, and by the early nineteenth century gooseberry-growing had become a cult amongst cottagers in the industrial north and Midlands. At the end of the century 2,000 named varieties were in circulation.[20]

Cloudberry in flower high in the Cairngorms.

Traditional Oldbury tarts, from Oldbury-on-Severn in Gloucestershire, were reputedly made from wild gooseberries – though, being cooked for the Whitsuntide Fairs at the end of May, they must have been made from preserved, not fresh fruit. They were small raised pies, teacup-sized, filled with gooseberries and brown sugar. They are still occasionally served (made from cultivated fruit) in restaurants in the Severn Vale.

Cloudberry, *Rubus chamaemorus* (VN: Noop, Nowtberry). A subalpine shrub, confined to mountain bogs and moors north from Derbyshire and North Wales. The fruit – like an orange dewberry – rarely forms in Britain (unlike Scandinavia), because of an overwhelming preponderance of male plants. Cloudberries were so hard to come by in the Berwyn Mountains that in the parish of Llanrhaiadr anyone bringing a quart of the berries to the parson on the morning of St Dogfan's (the parish saint) Day would have his tithes remitted for the year.[21]

Cloudberries rarely fruit in Britain.

It is not easy to see another reason why anyone should scour the mountains for them. They make a thin marmalade, but are indifferent eating. As one North Yorkshire contributor puts it: 'They are known as "nowtberries" here because they taste of nowt! I tried to get up Noughtberry Hill one day in July, but was driven back by a heath fire. When I did get there two years later, the cloudberry plants had completely smothered the whole area.'[22] (Grigson finds a less entertaining but probably academically more correct explanation of the Northern 'knout'/'nowt' prefixes in the Middle English word 'knot', meaning a hill. And 'cloud-' originates from Old English *clud*, also meaning a hill, rather than from evocative moorland mists.[23] Names, like fruit, ripen with age.)

Raspberry, *R. idaeus*, is locally common on heaths and in open woods throughout Britain, often appearing in large colonies after clear-felling or coppicing. It is a native shrub, though in waste ground and near habitation it may be naturalised from garden varieties. The canes grow to about six feet, spread by suckering, and tend to die back after they have fruited in their second year. The familiar orange-red fruits are usually ripe by July, and at this stage they come away very easily from their pithy core, known as the hull. (I have picked them as late as October, though, from canes sheltered by, but growing through, a bramble patch, so that a single bush appeared to be bearing two different kinds of fruit.)

It is not hard to see why the raspberry has been the *Rubus* species taken most extensively into cultivation, given that its canes are virtually spine-free and spread with more restraint than brambles. The most successful cultivation and hybridisation is carried on in Scotland, whose climate seems to suit the plant; and some of the new varieties – together with naturally occurring hybrids and sports – are well established in the wild north of the border. A yellow-fruited form grows on Speyside.[24]

Loganberry, *R. loganobaccus*, is naturalised on railway embankments, commons, old allotments and waste places. It is one of a number of crosses between raspberry and blackberry species (including, more recently, the tayberry and boysenberry) which may occur spontaneously in the wild. **Salmonberry**, *R. spectabilis*, from North America, is

Blackberries, the one fruit still widely gathered from the wild.

grown chiefly for the ornamental value of its pink flowers and is naturalised in a scatter of woods and hedgerows. A promising sport of this – very tall, with mauve flowers – is the most likely identity of a *Rubus* found growing wild by a contributor near Dunbar, East Lothian: 'I was surprised when the berries ripened on the 15th June, about three weeks before the raspberries. The berry was almost identical, except in size and colour. It was bright orange and bigger than a wild raspberry, but smaller than the cultivated ones in a local farm. I would say that the biggest of the berries would be about the same size as the biggest of the wild brambles. It has a pleasant taste, although the jam that I made from 3 lb of them is not as good as the better-known

73

ones. Some of the plants are much taller than me, indeed one is about 12 feet tall. The berry comes off the hull cleanly.'[25]

Bramble or **Blackberry** species, *R. fruticosus* agg. (VN: Black heg, Blegs). Blackberrying is the one almost universal act of foraging to survive in our industrialised island and has a special role in the relationship between townspeople and the countryside. It is not just that blackberries are delicious, ubiquitous and unmistakable. Blackberrying, I suspect, carries with it a little of the urban dweller's myth of country life: harvest, a sense of season, and just enough discomfort to quicken the senses. Maybe the scuffling and scratches are an essential part of the attraction, the proof of satisfying outdoor toil against unruly nature.[26] It is a tradition going back thousands of years (blackberry seeds have been found in the stomach of a Neolithic man dug up at Walton-on-the-Naze, Essex), but in these times of increased fencing-off of whole areas of countryside, it is looked on with hostility by some landowners: 'One West Midlands farmer didn't like "townies" coming and "stealing" his blackberries. He wrote to the *Birmingham Post* advising other farmers to follow his example and put up signs saying the berries had been sprayed with poison.'[27]

But it can be a connoisseur's pastime, as well. Over 400 microspecies have been recognised in Britain, each one differing subtly in fruiting time, size, texture and taste. In some varieties you may detect hints of plum, grape, apple or lemon. Dave Earl of Southport, Lancashire, has drawn up his own gourmet's list:
'Perhaps the commonest bramble in the North-west is *Rubus tuberculatus*; whilst the fruits can be pleasant, they resemble those of *R. caesius* [the dewberry, see below] in consisting of a few large drupelets, and it is quicker to gather well-formed fruits. Some of the smaller fruiters can be very seedy and sour … One of the best is *R. dasyphyllus*, a common species of the hills, the flavour being pleasantly sweet. Of course flavour is very variable and I find that this can vary from sour to sweet to watery on the same panicle. I have often been put off eating the berries of the cultivated *R. procerus* for this reason. Nevertheless, with a good few ounces of sugar and some stewing they are ideal for jam and pie fillings. I much prefer the berries of *R. nemoralis* to those of *R. procerus*.

The bramble, from a herbal made probably at Bury St Edmunds Abbey in the eleventh century and which contains some of the earliest naturalistic plant drawings.

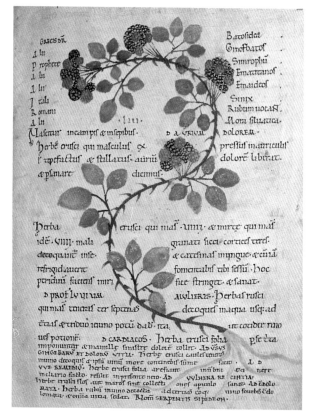

The fruits are of good size and flavour, and the species is common on acid soil, particularly on the site of former mosslands. If you are particularly hungry, *R. gratus* has large berries ... Members of the Wild Flower Society recently enjoyed feasting on the berries of bushes on Carrington Moss, Greater Manchester. This was despite the fact that the bushes grew along the perimeter fence of the gas works. The taste topper for me, however, was *R. bertramii*, encountered on Ashton Moss, Ashton-under-Lyme, in August 1993. There are only a few bushes there, but a good stand can be found at the north end of Knutsford Heath in Cheshire. Some bushes are very local in distribution. The "Bollin Blackberries", known to my grandparents and picked by myself as a child to make Auntie's crumble, were not described until 1971.
R. distractiformis – "from the north banks of the River

Bollin, Hale" – was named by Alan Newton, the expert who identified most of the brambles in the Liverpool Museum Herbarium. Even though this bramble had not been described as a distinct species, my Aunt preferred *R. distractiformis*.'[28]

Blackberries form in clusters at the end of mature shoots, which die back after two or three years' fruiting. The berry at the very tip of the stalk is the first to ripen, and the sweetest and fattest of all. A few weeks later, the other berries near the end ripen. These are less juicy, but fine for pies and jams. By the end of October, the remaining berries have often picked up mildews and bacteria and turned sour or cloying. There is an old saw (still widely known) to discourage picking these late, inferior specimens which says that the Devil pisses, or spits, on the blackberries on Michaelmas Night.

Earlier this century, wild blackberries were sometimes picked commercially, as in Somerset and Oxfordshire:

'They were collected by local children for sixpence a pound. They were used for dye. The money usually financed trips to the fair.'[29]

'In Eynsham, Oxfordshire, fruit was picked and sold to Coopers Marmalade of Oxford, who had the contract to make jam for the troops in the First War. Lots of local people did this to earn a few pennies. The fruit was taken into Oxford in an old pram.'[30]

Recipes are legion: old – such as blackberry crowdie, made with toasted oats, cream and rum; modern – blackberry vinegar, with the berries marinated with sugar in white vinegar and served with grilled goat's cheese; and instant – apple and blackberry sandwiches.[31] The most delicate is a junket, invented I imagine for the very young or very old, made simply by squeezing the juice from some very ripe berries and allowing it to set overnight in a bowl in a warm room. The result is the pure, ethereal essence of blackberry, hanging between liquid and solid.[32]

Bramble is also, of course, both loathed and respected for its thorns and powers of entanglement. Bushes were once planted on graves, to cover less sightly weeds and deter grazing sheep, but probably also as an echo of more ancient and magical hopes of keeping the dead in and the Devil out: 'The Old Man of Braughing can sleep in peace. For once more the villagers have completed the traditional ceremony of sweeping Fleece Lane and putting brambles on the old man's grave. The "old man" died at a ripe old age and the bearers were carrying his coffin down Fleece Lane to the churchyard when they stumbled on some stones and the coffin lid fell open and broke. The Old Man sat up and soon afterwards was married again. When he eventually died he left cash for Fleece Lane to be swept clean of stones each year and for brambles to be placed on his grave to keep the sheep off.' (Hertfordshire, 1957) [33]

In a churchyard in Cheshire the grave of a nineteenth-century bramble expert is adorned, deliberately or by happy accident, with a bush of *R. laciniatus*, a cut-leaved species of unknown provenance: 'In the village of Lower Peover there is in the churchyard an impressive tombstone of the Warren family. It has an unusual bramble planted in the grave and a stylised version carved up the tall stone. J. B. L. Warren [Lord de Tabley] wrote *The Flora of Cheshire* in 1899. He took a special interest in the *Rubus* family. It is good to see such a potent memorial to his great work.' [34]

The long, arching stems of bramble (and wild roses) were once known as 'lawyers' because of the trouble you have escaping if you happen to fall into their clutches. [35] An especially vicious form in Honeypot Wood, Norfolk, has been nicknamed '*Rubus Boadicea*'. [36] But they were apparently looked on more kindly by Victorian men of a romantic bent, because of the excuse they gave for paying attention to ladies' long skirts. The Pre-Raphaelite poet Thomas Woolner introduces them as welcome obstructions in his epic 'My Beautiful Lady' (1863):

> We thread a copse where frequent bramble spray
> With loose obtrusion from the side roots stray,
> And force sweet pauses on our walk.
> I lift one with my feet and talk
> About its leaves and stalk.
>
> Or maybe that some thorn or prickly stem
> Will take prisoner her long garment's hem:
> To disentangle it I kneel,
> Oft wounding more than I can heal,
> It makes her laugh, my zeal.

The succulent, white-bloomed fruit of the dewberry.

The ambivalent image of the bramble patch, simultaneously grasping and protective, permeates even the technical and supposedly rational business of woodland management. Despite bramble being an entirely natural component of woodland vegetation, waxing and waning according to the light allowed it by the tree canopy, commercial foresters attack it ruthlessly, in the belief that it 'smothers' young trees. Traditional woodland managers can view it rather differently: 'Bramble has been the saviour of our working coppices in Suffolk, as it has given vital protection to young coppice shoots (especially small-leaved lime) from the attentions of deer. As a consequence it is encouraged where browsing pressure is high.'[37]

Dewberry, *R. caesius*. Dewberries are quite common in hedge-banks, woodland edges and scrub, especially in damp places on calcareous soils. They have a low arching growth and can be recognised immediately by their berries, which have a few large drupes covered with white bloom, like miniature grapes. They are so juicy that they are difficult to pick. Snipping off a few berries with scissors or secateurs is the answer, after which they can be eaten like cocktail cherries, on their own sticks.

Wild strawberry, *Fragaria vesca*.
'As a child in the Yorkshire Dales I collected lots of wild strawberries on our evening walks before going to bed. In the morning we had wild strawberries with our breakfast cereals. When I returned to school we were asked to talk

about our holidays. I spoke about my camping holiday and described all the plants and flowers and the delicious wild strawberries. My class teacher listened in disbelief and said, "There is no such thing as a wild strawberry. It must have been from a garden." I was ridiculed by him for exaggerating and felt humiliated. But I wondered how you could get a cultivated strawberry if there were no such thing as wild strawberries!

Wild strawberries, often found lurking under leaves and in flavour often superior to cultivars.

I still find lots around the country on our walks. My three children know the story of the wild strawberry that doesn't exist. The first one we find each year gets special treatment as we joke about its not existing and then eat it!'[38]

This nine-year-old's logic is still lost on many people, who believe that any edible fruit growing wild is a garden escapee, or some kind of degeneration from an original cul-

tivated variety. Our native strawberry is not a direct ancestor of modern commercial varieties, but is a species in its
own right, and in flavour often superior to cultivars. In
limestone areas such as the Derbyshire and Yorkshire Dales,
the fruits are often warmed by heat reflected from the rock
and become soft, fragrant beads of sweet juice. (I have seen
a sixteenth-century recipe for a form of strawberry short-
cake, made with almond flour and cooked simply by leaving
the paste in the hot sun for a couple of hours.) Wild strawberries are very delicate when ripe and are easily bruised if
gathered directly into a basket or jar. In Sweden, they thread
them individually onto long grass stalks.

They occur quite commonly in open woodland and
scrub throughout Britain, especially on calcareous soils. In
parts of Gwent they are sufficiently common to have places
named after them, for instance Cwmsyfiog – 'Strawberry
Vale' – near Tredegar.[39] The plants often appear in large
quantities after felling in the southern beechwoods, especially where the soil has been disturbed. In Sussex and
Hampshire, 'strawberry slidders' were features of steep
woods where the felled trunks had been dragged downhill.
These eruptions are partly from buried seed, suddenly
exposed to the light. But the species spreads chiefly by run-

*A detail from
William Morris's
'Strawberry Thief'
design, inspired by
the wild fruit.*

ners, which can extend very quickly among its glossy, trefoil leaves.

Wild strawberry also finds sunny railway embankments a congenial habitat: 'We gathered wild strawberries into jam-jars from the "batters" – the banks of the railway lines between Kirkby Lonsdale and Kirkby Stephen. Strawberries flourished on the stony, well-drained slopes.'[40]

I have been shown white-berried strawberries growing on the rubble of disused railway lines. But the fruit is almost tasteless, and after a couple of years reverts to its normal colour. Altogether more interesting is the robust form known as the alpine strawberry, which will go on fruiting until the first frosts. It may have been one of these that Gilbert White picked 'ripe ... on a bank' at Selborne on 10 January 1790, after an exceptionally mild winter.[41]

Strawberries are represented in several churches, notably in St Mary's, at Whalley in Lancashire, where both leaves and berries are figured on a misericord, their respective shapes echoed by hop leaves and fruit on the supporters.[42] They also inspired William Morris: 'He was sitting in Kelmscott Manor courtyard, and noticed a thrush swoop down and take a wild strawberry in its beak. He rushed indoors and designed the famous "Strawberry thief" pattern. The wild strawberry patch is still there.'[43]

Garden strawberry, *F.* × *ananassa*, is the cultivated strawberry, bred chiefly from American wild species and occasionally naturalised on rubbish-tips, waysides and (like its wild cousins) railway embankments: 'I have found garden strawberries growing on the edge of railway lines near Patney and Etchilhampton, presumably from the pips of fruit thrown from passing trains.'[44]

Rose-hips (VN: Heps, Itchy-coos). The oval red fruits of wild roses have long been used as food. Gerard speaks of them making 'most pleasant meates and banketting dishes, as Tartes and such like'.[45] In the eighteenth century they were made into a purée, by the laborious process of slitting the fruits in half, cleaning out the pith and seeds, leaving the shells to soften (without cooking) and then rubbing them through a sieve.

During the Second World War, rose-hips came into their own in the form of rose-hip syrup, whose taste all wartime children can recall as vividly as dried egg. Nutritional scien-

tists had known since the 1930s that wild hips had a higher proportion of vitamin C than any other common fruit or vegetable. (A cup of rose-hip pulp provides more vitamin C than 40 fresh oranges.) But it wasn't until the war began to disrupt our usual sources of the vitamin (especially citrus fruits) that the Government began seriously to consider the use of rose-hips. In 1941 the Ministry of Health initiated a scheme for voluntary collection. One hundred and twenty tons were gathered that year for processing into syrup and distribution to small children. By the end of the war, by which time the collection was being co-ordinated by the County Herb Committees, the annual harvest was averaging over 450 tons.

Rose-hips, known locally as heps and itchy-coos, and used in the making of that wartime staple, rose-hip syrup.

Schools, scout troops, guide companies and children's gangs all took part, and many contributors remember the expeditions in late summer (the hips had to be collected when they had just turned red, to maximise the vitamin C content) and hauling the sackfuls back to the local school or village hall. With collectors being paid 3d a pound, some entrepreneurial youngsters were able to earn more than just pocket money.

The picking was encouraged most in the north of England, where the hips reputedly had a higher vitamin content, but storage sometimes became a problem: 'One year, on the children's first morning back from the holidays, the teacher sat down at the piano to play the opening hymn of the morning assembly. Her hands fell with a flourish on the keys, but not a sound came forth. Inspection revealed that in the holiday-quiet schoolroom mice had busied themselves eating fleshy bits of rose-hip and stuffing the seeds beneath the piano keys until they were packed solid!' (Cumbria)[46]

Collecting hips for National Rose Hip Syrup went on until the early 1950s. It was sold at a controlled price of 1s 9d per 6-oz bottle, though mothers and children were able to obtain larger quantities, at reduced prices, from welfare clinics. (It is still made commercially today, though from farmed 'wild' roses.)[47]

But many country-dwellers made (and still make) their own syrup, often following the precise instructions given by the Ministry of Food in their booklet *Hedgerow Harvest*.[48] The process involves mincing, stewing and then, crucially, straining through a jelly-bag to remove the prickly seeds, which can be a dangerous internal irritant. Boiled again with sugar and reduced, the hips make a bright red syrup which has been used for drinks, mousses and summer puddings.[49]

As for the seeds, they weren't an entirely useless by-product, as generations of children have known of their potential as an itching powder:

'I was a schoolmaster till 1987, and rose-hips were still being used then. It is not in fact the seeds that are used but the hairs attached to the seeds and the lining of the hip.'[50]

'During the late 60s, children in Dundee continued the tradition of using rose-hip seeds from the dog-rose and also ornamental roses planted in urban landscaping as itching powder. This activity is well recorded (although I suspect the effects are largely psychosomatic). However, I have never seen recorded anywhere the name applied by children to the seeds, the hips, and even the whole plant – "Itchy-coos". The second half of the name (translated as "cows") is a complete mystery but the term seemed to be quite widely used.' [51] (In the 1960s, the English rock group the Small Faces, for instance, sang about 'Itchy-Coo Park'.)

Blackthorn, *Prunus spinosa* (VN for fruit: Sloes, Slones, Bullums). The definitive account of the popular culture of the blackthorn – and one of the most vivid and concise biographies ever written of a native tree – was penned by William Cobbett more than 150 years ago:
'Everyone knows that this is a Thorn of the Plum kind; that it bears very small black plums which are called Sloes, which have served love-song poets, in all ages, with a simile whereby to describe the eyes of their beauties, just as the snow has constantly served them with the means of attempting to do something like justice to the colour of their skins and the purity of their minds ... These beauty-describing sloes have a little plum-like pulp which covers a little roundish stone, pretty nearly as hard as iron, with a small kernel inside of it. This pulp, which I have eaten many times when I was a boy until my tongue clove to the roof of my mouth and my lips were pretty near glued together, is astringent beyond the powers of alum. The juice expressed from this pulp is of a greenish black, and mixed with water, in which a due proportion of logwood has been steeped, receiving, in addition, a sufficient proportion of cheap French brandy, makes the finest Port wine in the world ... It is not, however, as a fruit-tree that I am here about to speak seriously to sensible people; it is of a *bush* excellent for the making of *hedges*, and not less excellent for the making of walking sticks and swingles of flails. The Black Thorn blows very early in the spring. It is a Plum and it blows at the same time, or a very little earlier, than the Plums. It is a remarkable fact that there is always, that is every year of our lives, a spell of cold and angry weather just at the time this hardy little tree is in bloom. The country people call it the *Black Thorn winter* and thus it has been called, I dare say, by all the inhabitants of this

Flower-frosted branches in a 'blackthorn winter'. Sloes follow in the autumn.

island, from generation to generation, for a thousand years.

This Thorn is as hardy as the White Thorn; its thorns are sharper and longer; it grows as fast; its wood is a great deal harder and more tough; it throws out a great deal more in side-shoots … The knots produced by these side-shoots are so thickly set, that, when the shoot is cut, whether it be little or big, it makes the most beautiful of all walking or riding sticks. The bark, which is precisely the colour of the Horse Chestnut fruit and as smooth and as bright, needs no polish; and, ornamented by the numerous knots, the stick is the very prettiest that can be conceived. Little do the bucks, when they are drinking Port wine, … reflect that, by possibility, for the "fine old Port" which

has caused them so much pleasure, they are indebted to the very stick with which they are caressing their admired Wellington boots.'[52]

Blackthorn is an abundant shrub of hedges, scrub and open woodland throughout Britain, and its reputation and uses have scarcely changed in the past century and a half:

'I firmly believe in the "Blackthorn winter" and have observed for over twenty years that the blackthorn has flowered during a bitterly cold spell of weather, usually after a "false spring".'[53]

The fertile cross between blackthorn and the cultivated plum, *P. × fruticans*, can produce thorns more than two inches long and tough enough to penetrate a tractor tyre.[54]

'Blackthorn thorns have a bad reputation for puncturing tractor tyres … They have a habit of producing patches of sucker growth. For example, many neglected hedges have spread out to become several yards wide. When these patches are cleared it leaves many sharp stubs and stumps, many between pencil and thumb thickness, and these can be sharp and hard enough to puncture a tyre. Blackthorn is a hard wood, so much so that "corkscrew" walking sticks of blackthorn are highly prized because they are so rarely found. (In contrast soft-stemmed shrubs and trees like sallow, aspen and birch are more readily deformed by twining honeysuckles.)'[55]

Blackthorn was also the traditional wood for Irish shillelaghs, once definitively described by the Chairman of the Pharmacology Department at the University College of Los Angeles as 'an ancient Hibernian tranquilliser'.

Sloe gin is now a more popular drink than imitation port and is traditionally made by gathering sloes in late September or October, pricking them with a skewer, half filling a bottle with them, adding a few spoonfuls of sugar and covering with gin. (Commercial sloe gin, made by Gordons in Britain, disappointingly uses east European fruit.) The purple, almond-flavoured liqueur is ready to drink by Christmas, but improves with age. When the liquid is finished the sloes can be eaten, neat or processed: 'As a by-product, the pitted, gin-soaked sloes can be dipped into melted chocolate, which is then allowed to set.'[56]

As one Sussex woman reported, 'My uncle had a saying: "He likes his women fast and his gin sloe." '[57]

Wild plums, *P. domestica* agg. (VN: Bully tree, Crixies, Winter crack). It is possible that the tree known as the bullace (*P. domestica* ssp. *insititia*), with large, sloe-like fruits, is native in woodlands in Britain. But its fruits are barely distinguishable from naturalised, dark-fruited damsons. And the many varieties of relict or bird-sown gages, 'prunes' and damsons that are found growing in the wild form such a continuous spectrum that they are best all treated generically as 'wild plums'. Many are the outcome of ancient crosses (accidental in some cases) between the blackthorn and various sweeter-fruited plum species introduced from Asia, in a lineage of Byzantine complexity. With such an ancestry it is no real wonder that feral plums are one of the best wild foods (many being edible straight off the tree, unlike sloes) and represent a huge genetic reservoir.

Most are to be found in hedges. They are sometimes deliberately planted, as windbreaks, pollinators or linear orchards. Some spring from bird-sown stones or discarded human picnics. Whatever their origins, they frequently spread by suckers.

'Plum appears to be one of the more persistent relic species which remain on the sites of long-deserted habitations. In Shropshire the species occurs near the sites of ruined cottages on common land, including The Cliffe and Clee Liberty.'[58]

'They were commonly planted in Kent as windbreaks for orchards. Nowadays supplanted by various kinds of poplar and European grey alder.'[59]

'In Suffolk, many old cottages have disappeared during agricultural development, or under wartime airfields. These old sites are often marked in the remaining hedgerows by cherry plum and bullace.'[60]

In Essex – round Dunmow, Harlow Common and Catmere End near Duxford, for instance – wild damsons, be they blue-bloomed, green or yellow, are known as 'crixies'.[61] At Edlesborough and Weston Turville, near Aylesbury, Buckinghamshire, two highly local varieties were used both for eating and for dye-making:

' "Edlesborough Prunes" were once prized in our parish for jam-making and for fresh fruit. During the Second World War they were sent to Covent Garden in crateloads. They provided the Parish with prosperity and ran alongside

Wild plums in the Lake District.

our Straw Plait industry. The Prune provided dye for the Luton hat trade. There are still old trees in the hedges, but they are falling down.'[62]

'The "Aylesbury Prune" is almost unique to Weston Turville, and I am told the fruit was used to produce an indigo dye for the colouring of the "pearl" pattern of straw plaiting which was a cottage industry here until the late nineteenth century.'[63]

'After the opening of the railway large quantities of fruit [Aylesbury Prunes] were sent all over the country and during the Second World War much jam was made for the men at Halton Camp, but the trade virtually ceased after the war.'[64]

Damson colonies in Staffordshire and Cheshire were also harvested to produce dyes for the Manchester cotton-mills and Stoke potteries:

'Damsons seem to occur in every garden and field around this area. This is explained by the local story that the fruit used to be collected by locals and brought by basket to the pottery firms in Stoke-on-Trent for use as a dye.'[65]

'The Burgh of Galashiels has a long association with wild plums, which recalls a successful skirmish against a band of Englishmen in 1337 just outside the town. The English were gathering wild plums when they were surprised and overcome by a group of local men who later called themselves the "sour plums of Galashiels".'[66]

But wild plums are not usually that sour. They can be used instead of cultivated damsons and greengages in pies and jams, or as sweeter substitutes for sloes in alcoholic cordials. An old recipe is for damson cheese, a thick, sugary jelly made from strained damson pulp, which was served as a condiment with cold meats. When the King of Nepal was on a state visit to Britain in the 1980s, he ordered a large quantity of damson cheese to accompany the roast lamb banquet he was throwing at London's Guildhall.[67] And an edible oddity I discovered one autumn in a hedge outside an orchard at Bourne End, Hertfordshire, was naturally sun-dried damsons. The hedge had been cut in late summer with the first plums already formed, and the trimmings lay beneath, covered with dry, wrinkled fruits that tasted exactly like thin-fleshed prunes.

Cherry plum, *P. cerasifera*, is the most readily distinguished of the true species, and the earliest flowering. The white blossom often appears as early as February, with or just a little before the glossy, bright green leaves. Cherry plum is native to south-east Europe and is widely planted and naturalised in hedges. Pure hedges of this species in the Chilterns and Vale of Aylesbury are characteristic of land owned (and settlements built) by the Rothschild family in the nineteenth and early twentieth centuries.

The fruit does not form often, but is red or yellow and crisp-fleshed.

Crab-apple, *Malus sylvestris* (VN for fruit: Scrogs). The true wild crab is a comparatively scarce tree of old hedges and woods, nothing like as common as the 'wilding' – the collective name for chance seedlings sprung from the pips of discarded domestic apples. Crab-trees are spinier than culti-vated varieties and, when mature, form trees with rounder and denser crowns. In hedgerows they can be conspicuous landscape features, especially when in blossom, and they are the third most mentioned species as boundary features in Anglo-Saxon and Welsh charters, occurring in nearly 10 per cent of 658 charters examined.[68]

Crab-apples are small, hard and sour, but make a good pickle, a pectin-rich base for jams, and the best of all wild fruit jellies, ranging in colour from yellow to deep pink, depending on the colour of the fruit. They can also be roasted and served with meat or added to warmed ale and winter punches. These are the crabs that 'hiss in the bowl' in Shakespeare's *Love's Labour's Lost*, and whose form the mischief-making Puck assumes in *A Midsummer Night's Dream*: 'And sometimes lurk I in a gossip's bowl,/ In very likeness of a roasted crab,/ And when she drinks, against her lips I bob'.[69]

The crab-apple was the most important ancestor of the cultivated apple, *M. domestica*. More than 6,000 named varieties of this have been bred over the centuries, of which probably only a third still survive. Because they must cross-pollinate to produce fruit, cultivated varieties do not come true from seed, and when a pip germinates it is likely to turn into anything, with genetic echoes, perhaps, from centuries-old ancestors. I know a green lane near Bovingdon in the Chilterns, not far from an area of one-time orchard land, in which there are three wilding trees, one with apples like

'Wilding' apple (sprung from discarded cores) on Cholesbury Common, Hertfordshire. The genes of many old – and possibly 'lost' – apples are preserved in the immense variety of wildings.

miniature Cox's Pippins, another whose fruit has a bitter-sweet, almost effervescent taste, like sherbet, and a scent of quince, and a third whose long, pear-shaped apples have a warm, smoky flavour behind the tartness, as if they had already been baked. On the shingle beach at Aldeburgh in Suffolk there is a prostrate apple of unknown provenance

Rowan (with juniper) at Little Langdale, Cumbria.

which bears fully ripe fruit before the end of June.

Wildings represent an extraordinary genetic reservoir in these days of mass-market fruit-growing, both of lost varieties and of potential new ones. Many of the most famous names in the apple dynasty came from such random springings, often in the most unpromising surroundings. Granny

Smith reputedly grew from an Australian woman's compost heap; Keswick Codlin from garden rubbish in Ulverston Castle; Shaw's Pippin from the council refuse tip at Wheathampstead in Hertfordshire.

Sometimes cultivated apples are deliberately set in the wild, echoing the frugal medieval practice of planting fruit trees in hedgerows or in the headlands at the end of the common fields:

'In this part of the world [Appleby (OE for 'apple village'), Cumbria] enclosure hedges were usually planted in the ratio of three thorns to one apple (very occasionally pear). There was a tremendous trade in hedging trees from "instant" nurseries all over the place. Any variety would do, and very rarely would the true crab be available, so our relics are the varieties of the time, and of cider pulp – any source of pips. We have not lost so many hedges up here as elsewhere in England, so many old ones survive. Immense variety of fruit is exhibited, by now scraggy and small, but I know of some I pick for culinary use. I work mainly with the MoD Forester for the North of England, on Warcop Army Range, where old trees persist. He is raising new stock from pips from old enclosure hedges.'[70]

'During the 1940s I spent several years in the Evesham district and had the pleasure of meeting an old countryman who looked after hedges. He told me that at the appropriate time of the year he would walk round with a pocket full of apple graftings. When he came across a suitable crab-apple stock, he would graft on a "proper" apple graft. Hence the large number of apple trees in hedges around Harvington, in particular.'[71]

Rowan, *Sorbus aucuparia* (VN: Mountain-ash, Witch wiggin tree, Keirn, Cuirn). Once widely planted by houses as a protection against witches, rowan is now better known as a street tree, a role it performs with civic efficiency. It has airy, ash-like foliage and orange-red berries, which only occasionally drop on pavements to annoy peevish pedestrians and car-owners.

It may have been the vivid colour of the berries that originally credited rowan with protective powers. Yet it was the wood that was regarded as the potent part of the tree. Up to the early years of this century, rowan boughs were hung over stables and byres in the Highlands, used for stirring cream in the Lake District, made into divining rods in Yorkshire, and cut for pocket charms against rheumatism in Cornwall.[72] In parts of Scotland there is still a strong taboo against cutting down a rowan tree, especially when it is close to houses.[73] The tree outside Gavin Maxwell's house at Camusfearna was famously cursed by the poet Kathleen Raine, with what Maxwell believed to have been disastrous consequences.[74]

But it is only on the Isle of Man that traditional rowan customs survive to any extent:

'In the Isle of Man [rowan] is still widely known as Cuirn. Apotropaic crosses of broken-off twigs … are still hung above the lintel of house doors (inside) on May Eve. Formerly these were used on animals, animal shelters, churns, etc.'[75]

'Two twigs about five inches long are plucked, never cut, and a split made in the centre of one with the thumb-nail. The other twig is pushed through and bound round with thread twisted by hand from sheep's wool taken from the hedge. If the wool is from the native Loaghtyn sheep so much the better. The cross is put up over the door of each

Sea-buckthorn berries, enjoyed by birds but underused by humans.

house, inside, fresh each year, on May Eve. On the same night it is as well to have primroses in the house. In more profligate days they would be strewn on the doorstep.'[76]

Magically protective or no, rowan's pale bark and brilliant berries make it a striking tree to find outside an upland farm, or framed against dark pines on an autumn heath. A fourteenth-century Irish poet wrote: 'Glen of rowans with scarlet berries, with fruit fit for every flock of birds; a slumbrous paradise for the badgers in their quiet burrows with their young.' ('Deirdre Remembers a Scottish Glen')[77]

Rowan berries are fit for humans, too, and with a few crab-apples make a sharp, marmaladish jelly traditionally served with game and lamb. The tree grows in woods and scrub throughout Britain, chiefly on acid or light soils, but sometimes on chalk.

Sea-buckthorn, *Hippophae rhamnoides*, is a spiny shrub, whose leaves and twigs are covered in silvery scales. It is a coastal species, native in sandy places along the eastern shorelines of England, but much planted elsewhere, to help stabilise dune-systems on the coast and, because of its salt tolerance, by urban roads and roundabouts.

In the autumn it bears bright orange berries, which are eagerly devoured by wintering thrushes and other migrant birds passing along the east coast. A Norfolk Flora notes: 'If it were not for bird-carriage, it would be difficult to account for the spread of this shrub along the whole of the Norfolk littoral.'[78]

The fruit has occasionally been used to make rather sharp jellies and preserves.

Elder, *Sambucus nigra* (VN: Boortree, Boontree, Borewood, Battery, Dog tree, Ellern, Fairy tree). It is hard to understand how this mangy, short-lived, opportunist and foul-smelling shrub was once regarded as one of the most magically powerful of plants. If you burned it, you would see the Devil. But, grown by the house, it also had the power to keep the Devil at bay. It could charm away warts and vermin. Until early this century drovers used malodorous elder switches to protect cattle from flies and disease, and hearse-drivers favoured elder-wood for the handles of their horse-whips – a telling and condensed symbol of centuries of jostling between superstition and practicality.

And this was by no means the only practical use. A mid-eighteenth-century farming encyclopaedia recommends elder as hedging in the kind of terms usually reserved for exotic spice trees: 'The Elder is the quickest of any in its shooting; and it will bear planting so large, and takes Root so easily, that it may be called an immediate Fence. To this let us add, that the Flowers and Berries bear a Price at Market; and that the Wood of the old Stumps is valuable, and of sure Sale to the Turners: and we shall find that there is great Reason for naming the Elder among the Hedge Shrubs, for that it equals any of them in Value.' [79] (And these 'elder fences' were not just workaday hedges, but were often planted in elaborate, criss-crossed double rows, so that the blossoms formed diamond patterns in June.)

Two centuries later a popular book on 'traditional' country crafts had just one sentence to spare on elder's place in the hedgerow economy: 'The unwanted wood such as elder and bramble is cut out.' The shrub is now widely regarded as little more than a jumped-up weed, a ragamuffin haunter of dung-heaps and drains.

Yet elder's image has always swung between the poles of veneration and distaste. Even its anatomy is ambivalent. It is too small to be a tree, yet too large and airy for a bush. Its root and heartwood are as hard as ebony, yet the young branches are weak, hollow and filled with insubstantial pith. The umbels of white flowers smell of honey, the leaves of mice nests. Having (like the nettle) a taste for rich, fertilised soils, it haunts graveyards and rubbish-tips. Yet it has always been regarded as one of the most bountiful sources of home medicine – 'a kind of *Catholicon* against all Infirmities whatever', as John Evelyn put it.[80] Even the name blurs magic and practicality. It is compounded from the Scandinavian tree spirit Hylde-Moer and Anglo-Saxon eldrun, derived from *aeld*, meaning fire, perhaps because the branches hollowed of their pith were used like bellows for blowing on fire, but must on no account be added to the flames.

Perhaps it was the contradictory qualities of elder that made it such a compelling and respected plant. It certainly needed a myth to account for the paradoxes, and in the Middle Ages it was declared to be the tree on which Judas hanged himself and, for the sake of mystical symmetry, also the tree of the Cross – which was why it became barely

Elder flowers can be eaten straight off the bush or fried in fritters.

capable of supporting its own fully-grown branches. ('Bour-tree, bour-tree, crookit rung,/ Never straight, and never strong,/ Ever bush, and never tree/ Since our Lord was nailed t'ye' is a stanza from a vernacular Scots verse. 'Bour' means pipe.)[81] Most of these myths have now disappeared. But some of elder's practical uses survive (one contributor said she would choose it as her 'desert island plant'),[82] and occasionally echo older practices mentioned by contributors:

'My husband – 50 years a farmer – recalls using the pungent elder leaves on the head bands of his working horses to keep the flies away. We had a large, low elder bush by the barn in the yard, and the cows used to rub under it in the summertime on their way into the cowshed for milking. One old cow would stay under there, given half a chance, when the flies were particularly bad.' (Kent)[83]

'As a youth my late father worked on the land, often handling horses. It was common practice to tie bunches of elder leaves to the harness to ward off flies.' (Essex)[84]

In Somerset and elsewhere, it was planted near dairies to keep flies away[85] – and by outside privies (though this may be a piece of retrospective explanation, since elder grows spontaneously in such places).

On the Isle of Man, 'tramman' 'was grown around houses to keep away evil spirits. If a girl washed her face in a lotion of tramman flowers and water it would make her beautiful.'[86]

Elder-flower water has retained a reputation as a skin-cleanser (one contributor recommends boiling the blossoms with cider vinegar),[87] and a refined commercial version is still sold as Eau de Sareau. It is also medically recognised as an eye-lotion.

But the principal use for the flowers and berries these days is as food. I find the flowers eaten straight off the bush as refreshing as ice-cream soda, but they are not to everyone's taste. In the war they were packed in barrels with salt to be used as a flavouring.[88] More popular are elder-flower fritters (known in Market Harborough as 'frizzets'),[89] made simply by dipping the freshly-opened umbels in batter and frying for a few minutes. The sweet muscat-flavoured flowers contrast wonderfully with the crisp batter.

Elder-flower cordial is made commercially at Woodchester near Stroud, using wild blossom harvested by part-time piece workers and infused with sugar-water.[90] So is elder-flower 'champagne', in Surrey, though the firm which produces this was ordered by the courts to cease using the name in 1994, after a case brought by the French Champagne association. It was felt that the use of the term for a wild-flower beverage would 'cheapen and debase' the reputation of true champagne. But the stuff itself is still regarded as one of the best 'country wines': 'Many farmers' wives still make elder-flower champagne – a quick and easily made summer drink, very popular at hay-making.'[91]

Back at the house, Lady Statham favours 'Lazy girl's pudding': 'Peel, core and slice thin two or three different varieties of apples and some very firm, practically unripe pears. Pour over it the following mixture – elder flowers steeped in a mixture of honey and hot water – and let your guests guess the ingredients.'[92]

'I like to eat, in effect, the flowers and berries at the same time: something which would have seemed impossible before the invention of the deep freeze. To do this I make a sorbet using the flowers and serve some with the last of the sorbet which was made from the berries during the previous autumn.'[93]

The berries by themselves also make a rich, dark wine, a 'rob' for sore throats, and are an ingredient of 'hedgerow jam'. They are also used in the making of a relish from the nineteenth-century gentlemen's club circuit, known as Pontack Sauce. Pontack's was a famous restaurant in London's Lombard Street, and its recipe for this tangy brew of elder-berries, claret, spices and onions was taken back to many country seats and adapted to the owner's idiosyncrasies. It was supposed to be kept for seven years before use.

The catalogue goes on. The pith inside the young stems is one of the lightest natural solids (with a specific gravity of 0.09, as against cork's 0.24). It is used commercially for gripping small biological specimens whilst they are cut for sections for microscopy. The stems from which it is scraped are of a surprisingly hard, pale, shiny wood which is very satisfactory to carve. A half-inch diameter elder twig can be whittled into a paper-knife in 20 minutes, by taking advantage of its already hollowed-out interior.

'On the Northumberland coast the "thowelds" or pins

for the oars were cut by the fishermen themselves from the "boontree" bushes which grew among the hedges. Apparently, this was a very greasy wood, which helped the oars to move freely. Identification of the boontree is difficult – opinion [and the name] suggests the elder.'[94]

The hollowed-out stems have also been made into a variety of peashooters and guns by generations of children:

'An elder gun was made from a hollowed-out stem, filled with a flexible twig (or a piece of clock spring) as a propellant.'[95]

' "Gun-skutes" were made. This was a sort of pop-gun made from hollow elder stems and a close-fitting stick.' (Isle of Man)[96]

'We produced guns for play from hollow elder bush stems, removing the pith except for a couple of inches at one end. The spring was a "steel" from corsets, which were in everyday use then by the village women. The steel was inserted in a loop. When firing at each other the hard seeds of goosegrass (locally named "clyders") were used.'[97]

'We used elderberries as ammunition in the peashooters to make a satisfactory bloody splodge. A handful of ripe elderberries squeezed on the wrist also produced a very believable stream of blood to alarm your Mum.'[98]

Finally, a note on 'touch-burners': 'In Sheffield my father introduced me to these home-made hand-warmers. A small, rectangular box of clay, say 2 by 4 by 1 inches internally, with a lid, sun-baked only, was half filled with "touch-wood" – in his case, the dry "tinder" of rotten elder wood. Onto this, a live coal or glowing piece of wood was placed; blown on until smouldering; then lidded and held in the hands. Sometimes, these hand-warmers worked for several hours.'[99]

Elder grows prolifically in hedgerows, woods (especially secondary woods), chalk downs, waste ground on enriched soils and abandoned cultivated land across Britain. It is, as one writer remarked, 'a typical product of contemporary life. It is light in construction, cheaply and rapidly produced, short-lived and either quickly repaired when damaged, or scrapped and replaced.'[100] It also has thousands of years of magical belief and peasant ingenuity behind it.

Kitchen Medicines

At some time or another, most of the wild plants of
Britain have been pressed into medicinal service.
Couch grass has been used for urinary complaints,
sanicle and bugle for ulcers and wounds, lesser
celandine for piles, borage for depression. Often these
are very personal remedies and their effectiveness
depends on the degree to which they are believed in.

But there are a handful of herbs – comfrey, feverfew and hop, for example – which seem to work with most sufferers and which have been validated by conventional medicine. These are the herbs that are concentrated on in this section. Also included are other domestically useful plants such as soapwort, which is used as the source of a mild detergent.

Pennyroyal, once a mainstay of folk medicine, but now reduced to a handful of pond-edges and damp commons.

'**Plant medicine**'. The use of wild plants in herbal and folk medicine is on the increase in Britain again – though it is, as ever, a highly subjective business. Personal faith, idiosyncratic sensitivities and mode of use all profoundly influence the results. Anecdotal accounts of successful remedies show that a large number of British plants have been used almost interchangeably to treat an equally large number of common disorders: almost anything will work with *someone* when it comes to dispelling bruises, warts and wind.

But there have been some discernible traditions, which have shaped the names, distribution and fortunes of many species. Most remedies must first have been discovered by trial and error, and species with quick, dramatic effects – purgatives such as buckthorn and narcotic sedatives such as henbane, for example – would have made their mark early. In more recent times, trial and error as a scientific discipline has brought a steady trickle of plant-based drugs into mainstream medicine – for example, aspirin from willow bark, colchicine (for gout) from meadow saffron, digoxin from foxgloves, and menthol from mints.

Yet from at least the early historic period many other plants with no obvious immediate effects on human physiology were also believed to have healing properties. It is hard for us to imagine the awe with which plants were held in a pre-scientific age. They could appear by apparently spontaneous generation. Barely distinguishable species could feed you, poison you or drive you mad. It is no wonder that all manner of theories were developed to explain and predict their effects. Astrology, scriptural interpretation and numerology were all pressed into service. But the most popular system was sympathetic magic. This was based on a search for analogy, association and pattern within nature, in the belief that like (or sometimes unlike) would cure like. Exterior similarities in shape, colour or texture were regarded as clues to inner resemblances. Processes of apparent cause and effect in the larger, visible world might generate similar processes deep inside living things. So parasitic plants such as mistletoe might 'overcome' human 'parasites' such as cancer. Ivy berries would cure drunkenness, because ivy strangles vines. Some classical authors even believed that notoriously windy food-plants such as lentil could protect (by repulsion) a garden from gale damage.

*Greater celandine,
from the collection
of flower paintings
prepared between
1828 and 1851
by women of the
Clifford family in
Frampton on
Severn.*

It is easy to mock these beliefs as primitive and super-
stitious, but at least they were based on observation and
an ecological outlook – of a kind. Sadly, in the expansive,
market-driven climate of the seventeenth and eighteenth
centuries, they began to be vulgarised by a new breed of
commercial herbalists into the notorious Doctrine of Signa-
tures. This decreed that all plants had been 'signed' by the
Creator with some physical clue as to their medicinal qualities. Yellow flowers were marked out for jaundice. The
blotchy, oval leaves of lungworts were ordained for diseased
lungs. Plants which rooted in stone (such as parsley-piert)
would break through kidney stones just as effectively.
Much of this, I suspect, was little more than an extravagant
brand of sales talk aimed at the gullible, analogous to the

Chelidonium majus Common Celandine

brandishing of scientific terminology in modern advertising. (Though sometimes it seems to have been a form of *aide-mémoire*, or a way of rationalising the properties of a plant whose effectiveness had already been proved by trial and error.) But the Doctrine was responsible for probably the bulk of the *materia medica* in the written herbal tradition, and its influence is still obvious on the lengthening shelves of herbal remedies in chemists' shops.

Yet there is a third strand of indigenous plant medicine, often overlooked in the written herbal tradition, in which both the above strands were rooted. 'Folk medicine' relies heavily on native plants, but is essentially an oral tradition, derived from hard-won experience mixed with family and local customs and a dash of superstition. Although the medicinal history of many plants is included in *Flora Britannica*, the evidence given here of current use is chiefly confined to this last category. Given the intensely local nature of the folk medicine tradition, it is surprising how much agreement there is about effective plants. There were some half a dozen species – including comfrey as a poultice for bruises, greater celandine as a wart-remover, dandelion as a laxative and diuretic, and feverfew for migraine – which were recommended from personal experience from all over Britain. And, it should be added, by mainstream practitioners, too.

Greater celandine, *Chelidonium majus*. The flowers of greater celandine would not immediately make you place it in the poppy family. They are custard-yellow and about the size of buttercups. But cut the stalk or leaves, and the latex characteristic of the family (orange in this species) oozes out. It is this that accounts for the 'chelidon' ('swallow') in its scientific name, and the plant is still called 'swallow-wort' in parts of North America, as it was by Lyte and Gerard in the sixteenth century.[1] There is a complicated myth, dating from classical writings and compounded in the medieval period, that swallows used the herb as a restorer of eyesight: 'It is called Celandine, not bicause it then first springeth at the comming in of the Swallowes, or dieth when they go away: for ... it may be founde all the yeere, but bicause some holde opinion, that with this herbe the dams [female swallows] restore sight to their yoong ones when their eies be out, the which things are vaine and false.'[2]

But sceptical though he might have been, Gerard was still slightly in thrall to sympathetic magic, and was not against recommending the highly corrosive latex for eye disorders in humans, 'for it clenseth and consumeth awaie slimie things that cleaue about the ball of the eie, and hinder the sight'. What it certainly did do was cause severe conjunctivitis in any unfortunate patient treated with it!

The latex also has a somewhat safer – and highly successful – role in herbal medicine as a wart-remover.[3] (Only comfrey and feverfew have more cures attested by our contributors.) This may have always been its role in folk medicine; and the reason it is so often found in rough ground close to buildings (it is especially fond of the foot of stone walls) may be because it was once a common plant in

Hop boughs are still hung on walls, especially in pubs in hop-growing areas. It is a purely decorative custom now, but echoes the old practice of hanging corn dollies in churches and farmhouses after harvest.

cottage physick gardens. It may even be a native, brought into gardens from open, disturbed habitats.

Oxford is greater celandine's heartland. It grows everywhere in this anciently stony city, at the edge of car parks, on old walls, in cloisters and at the foot of exclusive Fellows' staircases. Its lobed leaves are also unmistakably carved on the shrine to St Frideswide, which dates from 1289 and now sits in Christ Church Lady Chapel. Its presence is probably no coincidence, for Frideswide, as well as being the patron saint of the University, was also a benefactress of the blind. She was the daughter of a twelfth-century Mercian princess, and went into hiding for three years to avoid an arranged marriage. Her luckless suitor subsequently went blind, and, in an act of contrition, Frideswide became a nun. Not long afterwards, she summoned up a holy well in the village of Binsey, just upriver from Oxford. Its water was reputed to have miraculous powers, especially for eye and stomach problems, and this seems to have been the reason for her sanctification. So, when her shrine was carved, the prime eye-herb was added to the magnificent and precisely carved frieze of oaks (both species), hawthorns, ivy, hop, maple and sycamore – the only site in Britain where its image is recognisably carved in a sacred building.

Hop, *Humulus lupulus.* Hop's thick vines and bunches of cone-like fruiting heads are most familiar scrambling about hedgerows or – a favourite site – up telegraph poles and their stays. Often they are relics of old hop-gardens. But hop is almost certainly a native and haunts wilder habitats such as fens and river-banks too. In undisturbed and well-lit places the woody stems can stretch up to 20 feet in length. One plant in Kings Bromley, Staffordshire, was heavy enough to pull down a holly tree.[4]

Hop has the kind of deeply-lobed leaves beloved of stone- and wood-carvers, and it figures alongside white bryony, grape-vine, maple and buttercup on the medieval capitals of the Chapter House of Southwell Minster in Nottinghamshire.[5] The female flowers are carved there too, tucked under the leaves.

Hops are dioecious, bearing male and female flowers on different plants. The male flowers are small and green, but the female – likened by John Gerard to 'scaled Pine apples'[6]

Wild hops scrambling over a hedge in Hampshire.

– are large and unmistakable, and the source of the hop's essential oils. Each lobe of the cone-like structure is studded near its base with yellow glands, which exude a mixture of aromatic oils and resins known as lupulin. Their scent is quite distinctive, with hints of garlic and ripening apples and yeast, and it is no surprise that hops were used in herbal medicine long before they were employed in making beer. They were recommended as an appetite stimulant, a mild pain-killer and a sedative. It was a pillow stuffed with hops that finally cured George III's insomnia and popularised this sleep-aid: 'It was remarkable that the first favourable change was due to Mr Addington, not indeed in his political capacity, but rather in his filial capacity. He remembered to have heard from his father, an eminent physician, that a pillow filled with hops would sometimes induce sleep when all other remedies had failed; the experiment being tried on the King was attended with complete success.'[7] More recently, infusions of hops, used as mild tranquillisers, were included in British and American Pharmacopoeias well into the 1900s, and hop pillows are still widely made and sold.

Hops were not introduced as a bittering agent in brewing until the end of the Middle Ages. Even then other wild plants were still often used to preserve and flavour ale – notably bog-myrtle, wormwood, costmary or 'alecost', and ground-ivy or 'ale-hoof'. But hops enabled the brew to be kept longer, and 'beer', flavoured with hops, began to be distinguished from 'ale', made without them. By the end of the sixteenth century beer was the more popular English drink, and hop-growing spread over many areas of southern England and the Midlands. It may have been this expansion that gave rise to another use for the plant – eating the young shoots. But it was in the late nineteenth century, when large numbers of families from London's East End used to migrate down to the Kent hop-fields to help with the pruning and picking, that hop shoots earned a wider popularity. Bundles of the young pruned shoots were boiled like thin asparagus.

There is a custom in hop-growing areas of hanging a bough of hops on a wall or over the fireplace.[8] In Hampshire I have seen boughs hung over the bar in pubs.

Bog-myrtle, *Myrica gale* (VN: Sweet gale, Gold withy). Bog-myrtle is a shrub of wet, acid heathland and moors, chiefly in Scotland, North Wales and north-west England, but with surviving populations in, for instance, the Devon and Surrey commons and the Norfolk Broads. It is rather drab in appearance, enlivened by the stubby orange-brown catkins in spring and early summer. But the whole plant emits a resinous, balsamic fragrance, especially when in flower. And in sites where there are large colonies, for example in damp valleys and by streamsides in the New Forest, the scent is astonishingly pervasive. It can carry hundreds of yards, and the aromatic substances responsible are occasionally blamed for tainting milk. In fact sweet gale is rarely browsed and flourishes best at the junction between grazed areas – such as the New Forest 'lawns' – and the heath proper, where competition from grasses is less.

'When my family first came to the New Forest in 1923, we found that the local name for bog-myrtle was "Gold Withy" (literally golden willow). The plant, common in Forest bogs, was blamed for giving a peculiar flavour to the milk of cows which ate it.'[9]

More often bog-myrtle has been both admired and used for its scent. 'Gale' is commemorated in several place names, for instance Galsworthy in Devon, 'the slope of the bog-myrtle'.[10] The aromatic resins have been used for scenting candles, and the whole plant is still used in brewing and cooking and as an insect repellant.

'Gale beer is a drink traditionally made from bog-myrtle. But the tradition of using the fragrant wax in candles is lost with the art of making tallow candles.'[11]

'Grows in wet places on the edge of the North York Moors. The very pleasant aromatic odour of this plant is added to home-made beer by mixing the leafy branches with the hot liquid in the early stages of the beer-making process.'[12] (The Gale Inn at Littleborough, over the border in Lancashire, is apparently named from the plant's use in beer, though the plant itself has vanished from the region.)[13]

'In Islay and Jura it was used as a garnish for food and stored with linen as a means of driving away moths and finely scenting the cloth.'[14]

'In Sutherland we are proud to still have small areas of bog-myrtle. When put in sachets with clothes, laundry, or blankets, its scent is as delightful as that of lavender. Insects

Bog-myrtle in damp heathland on Hartland Moor, Dorset.

do not feel attracted to it, especially moths. Some people, especially anglers, even wear a sprig in a button-hole against midges.' [15]

In 1995 a commercial midge-repellant based on bog-myrtle appeared on the market under the name 'Myrica'. It was produced from wild myrtle gathered by crofters on the Isle of Skye, which was then steam-distilled to produce a volatile essential oil. The initial trials vindicated the plant's folk reputation. Eight volunteers each had one arm covered in a gel made from the essential oil and the other left untreated. Over 10 minutes, the untreated arms recorded 155 bites while the treated arms received just 13.

Soapwort, *Saponaria officinalis* (VN: Bouncing Bett – especially applied to the double-flowered form). There is no wishful thinking in this name. Soapwort is a detergent-herb, plain and proven. Simply rubbing a leaf between the fingers will produce a slight, slippery froth. Boiled in water, the plant produces a green lather with the power to lift grease and dirt, especially from fabrics. The detergent effect is due to the presence of saponins – chemicals which, like inorganic soaps, appear to 'lubricate' and absorb dirt particles.

Soapwort's properties have been exploited across Europe and the Middle East, where it is native. It has been cultivated for laundering woollens in Syria, used as a sheep-wash prior to shearing in the Swiss Alps, and in Britain employed as a soaping agent by medieval fullers, who beat the finished cloth to clean and thicken it (one medieval name was 'foam dock'). And because vegetable saponins are so much gentler than soaps, *Saponaria* has been used much more recently for washing ancient tapestries. 'The natural silk produced by the Hart-Dyke family [and destined for royal wedding dresses] was washed with this vegetable detergent.' [16] In the Victoria & Albert Museum it was last used for cleaning fragile fabrics in the 1970s. The National Trust have also used it, for bringing up the colours in antique curtains. [17]

Although soapwort may be native along rivers in parts of south-west England and North Wales, some colonies are probably relics of this ancient use in laundering, especially when they grow by the sites of old mills: 'Just outside the churchyard at St Winnow, beautifully situated on a tidal creek of the River Fowey, there was a mass of soapwort until the site was developed. The soapwort has gone for ever, but I cannot believe that it was not originally planted for one of its important uses, the washing of church vestments, and with the tidal river nearby.'[18]

But most soapwort, on road- and rail-sides and waste ground, originates from more mundane garden throwouts. This is especially true of the decorative double variety, *flore pleno*, which – in honour of the species' long association with exuberant washerwomen – is known on both sides of the Atlantic by the splendid name of Bouncing Bett.

Broad-leaved dock, *Rumex obtusifolius* (VN: Docken, Dockan). An abundant perennial of fields, gardens and waste places, still universally used, by children especially, to rub on nettle stings.

'A new name invented by my son when he was three is "doctor leaf" for dock, which is what he thought we were saying because it makes nettle stings better. The name has been used by us ever since.'[19]

Broad-leaved dock, a common target for weedkiller sprays, but still widely used for rubbing on nettle stings.

'When my friends and I were out exploring the woods and fields we'd often take a bottle with "potion" in it to put on any nettle or insect stings. This we made by chopping up dock leaves and lemon-balm leaves and shaking in water.' [20]

It has also been used as a more serious salve by adults: 'My grandmother's practice was to collect young dock leaves before breakfast. These were still wet with dew. They were thoroughly washed before being added to pure melted pigs' lard in a stout saucepan. The mixture was allowed to reduce on a low heat until the residue was a pale green colour, after which it was strained into clean jars and, when set, sealed. This ointment was used for the treatment of piles.' [21]

'Still the best antidote to nettle stings. Works perfectly on dogs' feet, too (one of our dogs is sensitive to nettle stings).' [22]

In Lancashire it has also been used 'for cleaning dogs' backsides', and in Sussex for protecting dairy products from the heat, like butterbur, an ancient practice which gave broad-leaved dock the obsolete name of 'butter dock': 'My mother (who made Cheddar cheese and butter in her youth) used dock leaves to keep butter cool in the summer. They were draped over the dish, which was kept in cool water.' [23]

Comfreys, *Symphytum* species, are a small but difficult group, variable in themselves and prone to hybridisation. The three commonest species, below, tend to be used interchangeably in herbal medicine, etc. **Common comfrey**, *S. officinale*, is a bushy perennial with bristly leaves and spear-shaped, reticulated leaves. The flowers are pale cream or purplish and hang in bell-like clusters. It is a native, locally frequent by streams and rivers, in fens and ditches and on damp roadsides and waste ground. **Russian comfrey**, *S. × uplandicum*, is found in similar habitats and is now the commoner plant. It is a cross between common comfrey and **Rough comfrey**, *S. asperum*, and was probably first introduced to Britain as a fodder plant. The flowers are blue to violet or purplish when open. It back-crosses with *S. officinale*, forming a range of intermediate types. **White comfrey**, *S. orientale*, was introduced from west Russia and Turkey and is naturalised in hedgerows, churchyards and waste places, chiefly in eastern and southern England.

(VN for all species: Knitbone, Nip-bone, Ass-ear.) As can

Comfreys are common waste-ground and wayside species, much used in herbal medicine for healing wounds.

be guessed from its surviving common names, comfrey is still used as a healing poultice, for sprains, bruises and abrasions, and with more apparent success than almost any other herbal medicine. In this respect its users are carrying on a tradition which goes back to classical times. Comfrey (probably a corruption of the Latin *conferva*, a healing waterplant mentioned by Pliny, whose name is related to the verb *confervere*, to grow together) contains a substance called allantoin, which promotes healing in connective tissue. The medieval herbalists knew the plant as 'bone-set', and the root was lifted in spring, grated and used much as plaster of Paris is today. The whole plant was regarded as a master-healer and was used for everything from drawing splinters to easing backache.

Today, the uses are just as various and range from emergency backwoods first-aid to relieving the sting of a hard catch in a village cricket match.[24]

'After a chain-saw accident I cycled four miles to Riseley to get some comfrey roots. That ride was uncomfortable and opened up the gash even more. I dug some comfrey root and scraped the white flesh into a thick, jelly-like paste. I plastered this into the cut and topped it off with a piece of kitchen towel pushed into the jelly. After a while the jelly set into a stiff but yielding gel which held the edges of the wound together. I did nothing more with the cut, just left the comfrey in place until it and the sides of the cut had dried, at which time it more or less fell out. Within a couple of weeks only a surprisingly small scar could be seen.'[25]

'I work as a GP, and one of my patients had a coronary artery bypass recently. This was a very high-tech operation at the famous unit at Harefield Hospital. The lower end of the long leg wound failed to heal despite numerous standard dressings of different medical products. After an interval of a few days I visited the house to find a beaming patient. The leg wound was healed. He was delighted to tell me he had made an infusion of comfrey from his own garden plants (he is a town-dweller) and applied soft dressings soaked in the infusion.'[26]

'Conway Valley Nurseries had large quantities of Russian comfrey growing in an unused area in 1987. The owner told me that, prior to the First World War, the previous owner had cultivated this plant and that the leaves were transported to Manchester markets, where they were sold to cotton-mill workers for lining clogs to ease tired and aching feet.'[27]

'In the Yorkshire coalfields, comfrey poultices were used to treat what was called "beet knee" – purple, painful and unbearable to walk on, the reward of crawling in the low seams of the mine. Mother's remedy was the fresh leaves, boiled, drained slightly and then placed as hot as he [Father] could stand on the offending knee, and bandaged tightly on top to hold it in place. This indeed was a miracle cure, the swelling being reduced overnight and Father back at work without too much time off. I can still remember, 35 years on, helping Mum to pick those comfrey leaves and the exact location of the plant.'[28]

'My mother is in her eighties and when she came to visit us after breaking her wrist last year [1992] announced while unpacking, "I've bought some knitbone with me, to put on my wrist, that Elizabeth picked, up the lane." From these she made an infusion which she used to bathe her wrist.'[29]

Similar stories of use on ageing and arthritic joints come from many places, including an old people's home in Staffordshire.[30] Its use even extends to household pets: 'I used it in a poultice for a dog after a road accident – his fur grew back, so I used it on a bald guinea pig, whose fur also grew back.'[31]

The old practice of taking regular comfrey infusions or concentrated tablets internally for ailments such as gastric ulcers and colitis is now discouraged, as the plant contains alkaloids which can cause liver damage in large quantities. But the occasional young leaf eaten as a salad, or fried in batter as the German dessert Schwarzwurz, is unlikely to cause any problems. Comfrey was eaten quite widely in the Second World War.[32]

But probably the most widespread use of comfrey at present is as 'green manure'. Gardeners either grow it on the spot and dig it in or make a liquid feed from it: 'People are using it to make a practical tomato fertiliser by soaking a carrier bag full of the foliage in a big bucket of water until it goes brown and smells like animal manure.'[33]

Pennyroyal, *Mentha pulegium*, is a smaller, creeping species, with a very pungent odour. In folk medicine it was regarded as something of a panacea and widely grown in cottage gardens. It certainly has sedative and antispasmodic properties and, in large doses, had an underground reputation in the countryside as an abortifacient. Pennyroyal's habitat – the muddy edges of cattle wallows and village ponds – has declined dramatically over the past few decades, and it is now an endangered species, down to little more than a dozen sites, mainly in the south.

Wild clary, *Salvia verbenaca*. Not unlike cultivated sage, though less aromatic, wild clary grows in dry grassland, dunes and roadsides in southern and eastern Britain, and seems to have had a long affinity for churchyards, particularly in Suffolk and Sussex. The Revd Dr Frederick Arnold (author of *The Flora of Sussex*, 1887) suggested that this was the result of a medieval practice of sowing 'wild English sage' on graves, in the belief that it conferred immortality, and cited as his authority a twelfth-century aphorism: 'Why should he who grows sage in his garden die?' Arnold's interpretation seems rather perverse and it is more likely that the saying refers to the health-giving properties of clary for the *living*. (The Latin name *Salvia* is related to *salus*, 'health'.) In early herbal medicine it was a 'clear-eye', which became vulgarised to 'clary'. The seeds were soaked in water until they became mucilaginous, and the resulting jelly (rather like frog-spawn) was put in the eye to soothe and cleanse it.

Several other species of *Salvia* from southern Europe are naturalised in waste ground, including **sage** itself, *S. officinalis*, **clary**, *S. sclarea*, and **whorled clary**, *S. verticillata*.

Feverfew, *Tanacetum parthenium* (VN: Bachelor's buttons, Featherfew). As its name suggests, feverfew was a medicinal herb given for colds and fevers. In fact it was almost the classical and medieval world's aspirin, recommended for headaches, rheumatism, and general aches and pains. It reached Britain from its home in the Balkans some time during the early Middle Ages and is now widely naturalised by walls and old buildings and on waste ground and waysides close to cottage gardens. It has also become one of the great success stories in herbal medicine and had its reputation vindicated by work at the City of London Migraine Clinic. In 1978, after a newspaper story about a woman who had successfully rid herself of persistent migraine attacks by chewing feverfew leaves daily, many patients at the clinic

Feverfew, an ancient remedy recently vindicated by orthodox medicine. This is a golden-leaved variety.

began self-medicating with the leaves. Dr Stewart Johnson decided to undertake a long-term survey of some 270 feverfew-takers (partly to ensure that they were not doing themselves any harm). The results were remarkable. After a leaf a day for three months, 70 per cent reported a significant decrease in the frequency or severity of their attacks. A third appeared to have abolished their attacks altogether. These were far better results than had been obtained with any other form of preventative treatment, and they were confirmed by a more rigorous double-blind trial on a smaller sample of patients, using measured quantities of dried leaf made up into capsules.[34] The active chemicals have now been isolated and work by stopping blood vessels in the brain going into spasm, which is believed to be the

immediate 'cause' of migraine attacks. Many sufferers now make their own feverfew pills or sandwiches [35] or simply nibble the leaves: 'I am a migraine sufferer who takes feverfew and believes it really helps to reduce the frequency of attacks. I walk to work with my dog over the Malvern Hills each day, deliberately taking a route past a stone wall through the Whyche cutting (so called because it was the old salt road from Droitwich through to Wales) where feverfew grows abundantly. I browse on a fresh leaf or two every morning on my way down to the office.' [36]

Even without its medicinal properties, feverfew would be a welcome wayside plant – often becoming naturalised in its golden-leaved or double-flowered forms (the latter one of many plants known as 'bachelor's buttons') – with its foliage smelling bracingly of camphor.

Chamomile, *Chamaemelum nobile*. Chamomile seats, mossily soft and smelling of apples (or bubblegum to some modern young noses), [37] were a favourite feature of Elizabethan herb gardens, [38] and are currently enjoying a revival. There were even chamomile lawns, and it was on one such fragrant pitch that Sir Francis Drake is reputed to have played his famous game of bowls. But the feathery foliage needed regular clipping and de-flowering if the plant was to develop into a tight sward. It was not until the discovery of a non-flowering and less scrambling variety ('Treneague') in Cornwall earlier this century that chamomile lawns became a practical possibility in ordinary gardens.

But the chamomile lawn is not a human invention. The plant's natural habitat is tightly grazed cliff-top grasslands, sandy commons and damp woodland clearings, and it adapts to grazing by adopting a more or less prostrate form. Previously it occurred over much of England, though it was always commoner in the extreme south. But now, as a consequence of a general decline in grazing, especially of village greens and commons, it has become a scarce plant, confined to the south-west peninsula and the Hampshire and Sussex Wealds. Its natural strongholds are some of the commons and greens on the edge of Dartmoor and damp, pony-grazed glades in the New Forest, which are actually known locally as 'lawns'. But Heather Winship, who has studied the history and fortunes of chamomile, has found that, in Sussex particularly, it is flourishing in a comparatively new habitat – the cricket pitch. Very often these have been created on village greens which hold residual colonies of chamomile, and where the regular summer mowing and rolling mimic the kind of grazing pressure under which chamomile swards flourish. As a result the cricket grounds at Heyshott and Westbourne now support some of the healthiest populations of chamomile in West Sussex. It has also been found recently at the ground at Hartley Wintney, Hampshire, one of the oldest pitches in England, established on the village green in 1776.[39]

Dried chamomile flowers are used in a sedative tea.

Colt's-foot, *Tussilago farfara* (VN: Son-before-father, Foal's foot, Disherlagie, Dishylaggie, Tushylucky, Tushies, Baccy plant, Coughwort, Cleats). This is one of the earliest spring flowers, its cheerful, yellow blooms and scaly stems often appearing in February, a month or two before the leaves – hence 'son-before-father'. The plant's whole story is told by its common names. 'Colt's-foot' itself describes the hoof-like shape of the leaves, which are mealy above when they first appear and covered with white felt beneath. The Scottish 'tushylucky' and its variants are corruptions of the Latin *tussilago* – a name used by Pliny, related to *tussis*, a cough – which records the use of the leaves as a cough medicine (perhaps because of a slight similarity to lungs in their shape). Ironically, it has also been used as a substitute for tobacco. The dry felt on the leaves certainly smoulders well and has been used as tinder.

'It is used as herbal tobacco, and known as "Baccy plant" in Somerset.'[40]

'I have vivid memories of an itinerant farmworker who used to appear cross-country to gather the leaves of the coltsfoot which was prolific in just one triangle of our 20-acre orchard, presumably for selling as herbal tobacco.'[41]

'I remember eating coltsfoot rock in wartime because it came from the chemist and counted as a cough sweet and was therefore not "on the ration".'[42]

Colt's-foot grows in all kinds of waste, rough and cultivated places, especially where there is poor drainage.

Banes and Baubles

Not all active plants are medicinally or even domestically useful. Some of the most potent herbs – for example, birthwort and henbane – have fallen out of favour and are now regarded as poisons, while others, such as deadly nightshade, provide the raw materials for prescription medicines. Foxglove is a classic example of a powerful herb that was used

erratically (and often dangerously) by early herbalists, but which led to the refinement of an effective drug – in this case digitalis, for heart failure.

Other herbs have been used more light-heartedly. The roots of marsh-mallow have been made into teethers, and the poisonous berries of white bryony into a temporary necklace.

Foxgloves, the 'witches' thimbles' of medieval herbalists, standing their ground in the landscapes of the nuclear age.

Birthwort, *Aristolochia clematitis*. An intriguing perennial from southern Europe, once in wide use as a medicinal herb because of a fancied resemblance between its funnel-shaped yellow flowers and a uterus. Birthwort was given to speed up labour, and it would have been a standard herb in the gardens of abbeys where the nuns had midwifery duties, though it has never been accepted by orthodox medicine. But it also has more potent pharmacological properties. The distinguished Oxford botanist Professor E. F. Warburg was fond of scandalising audiences by describing birthwort as 'a good abortifacient, only found in England in nunneries, where it is an introduced plant'. Whether it was ever used to cover up rare indiscretions will probably remain a monastic secret. But Warburg's widow, Primrose, writes that a botanical friend heard from a Mother Superior that 'she'd got it round her nunnery and she'd needed it the previous year. History does not, unfortunately, say whether she *used* it.' [1]

In Northumberland it was also used by dairy farmers for expelling the afterbirth after a calf had been born.[2]

Most of the naturalised colonies of birthwort are – or were – on the sites of old abbeys or ecclesiastical establishments. Those at Bury St Edmunds Abbey in Suffolk, the twelfth-century almshouse of St Cross in Winchester and the Benedictine Carrow Abbey in Norwich have now gone. But the plant clings on amongst the nettles at the ruins of Godstow Nunnery outside Oxford, and in a few places in and near Cambridge, where it may once have been commercially cultivated.

Hemp, *Cannabis sativa* (VN: Marijuana, Grass, Pot, Ganja, Hash). Hemp is the source of the listed drugs marijuana (the dried leaves) and cannabis (the dried resin which exudes from the leaves and stem), and these days can be legally grown in this country only under Home Office licence. Previously it was cultivated both as a medicinal herb and as a source of fibre. Cannabis seeds have been found in the remains of the medieval Augustine Monastery at Soutra, East Lothian, and the plant was probably introduced there from the Middle East as a sedative.[3] It continued to be officially prescribed in this country as a tranquilliser (usually as 'Tinctura Cannabis Indicae') up until the 1930s, though this was prepared from imported plants. Naturalised plants usually sprang from spilt hemp

Birthwort, a relic of old monastic herb gardens, on the site of Godstow Abbey, Oxfordshire. It was used to speed up childbirth and occasionally as an abortifacient.

seed, which was used as a bird food and in anglers' ground-bait mixtures (which explains the plant's occcasional appearance along canal towpaths).

Now it is being cultivated again, for its fibrous qualities. By 1993 two farmers, one just outside Oxford and the other in Essex, had been granted licences and were together growing more than 1,500 acres of cannabis. The crop is used chiefly in the making of high-grade paper products, such as Bibles and, ironically, cigarette papers, and 'archive quality' paper, which doesn't degrade like that based on wood pulp.[4]

Marijuana sometimes sprouts from bird-seed in waste places.

Hemp and hops from a Tudor pattern book.

But any smoker wondering if potent material could be scrumped from these farms is likely to be disappointed, as cannabis strains grown for fibre develop little of the active narcotic ingredient (tetrahydrocannabinol) in our climate. Nonetheless, hopeful users have sometimes resorted to clandestine outdoor cultivation, as in a plot discovered in Ashdown Forest and perhaps the four plants found in a woodland clearing near Shrewsbury in 1980;[5] or they have picked the plants which still spring occasionally from bird-seed. Hemp seed is, strictly speaking, banned from such products. But now and then the odd unscreened seed slips embarrassingly through, as in a Hexham garden: 'An elderly friend feeds the wild birds regularly on her terrace outside a picture window. When we were visiting she pointed out a magnificent plant growing in the paving and said how excited she was that this lovely plant must have arrived in the birdseed. We told her what it was. Sadly for such a decorative plant she had to pull it up because she had the vicar and several ladies of the church coming to tea that afternoon.'[6]

Unfamiliarity with the fingered leaves of real cannabis plants no doubt lies behind some farcical cases of mistaken identity, in which, for instance, young conker trees have been impounded:

'During the summer of 1977, the Wiltshire Police carried out a drugs raid at my secondary school, looking for cannabis plants. They confiscated and left with a horse

Marsh-mallow, whose roots were once used to make the well-known sweet.

chestnut seedling in a pot, obviously not believing its owner that they would find a conker attached to the end of it.'[7]

'A Drug Squad descended on the Sussex Trust for Nature Conservation headquarters at Woods Mill without warning and without a search warrant. The squad had been tipped off that the Trust were growing cannabis. Many plants on the Trust's nature trail are labelled and no doubt someone with insufficient understanding had reported the inoffensive Hemp Agrimony, *Eupatorium cannabinum*, quite unrelated to cannabis.'[8]

Marsh-mallow, *Althaea officinalis*, is the plant whose roots were originally used to make the famous sweet. They were dug up from the marshes of the Thames estuary, and contain enough starch, sugars, oils and gelatinous matter to be turned into jelly simply by infusing them in water.

In France the dried roots (*hochets de guimauves*) are still sold in chemists as teethers. They have the advantage of growing ready-shaped for the job – they resemble thin pale carrots – and can be sucked like a dummy. They are hard and fibrous enough for a baby to chew on, but slowly soften as their mucilage is released (which, as a bonus, is calming to the stomach).

Now, in Britain at least, this is a declining species, its velvety, grey leaves and soft pink flowers a surprise to find along the brackish creeks and muddy paths of the south and east-coast marshlands.

White bryony, *Bryonia dioica* (VN: Mandrake, Wild vine). White bryony is the only native British member of the gourd or cucumber family, and in summer its greenish-white flowers, five-lobed leaves and coiled tendrils are very reminiscent of the greenhouse vegetable's. But there, any similarities end. In winter, bryony bears strings of green berries which turn a brilliant orange-red, and which – like the rest of the plant – are dangerously poisonous.

The most toxic part are the roots, which are white, succulent and often as much as six inches thick, with an acrid and bitter taste. Despite this, cattle are sometimes fatally attracted to them. A notorious case occurred in the 1960s, during the laying of a pipeline across pasture land. The operation entailed removing some 60 yards of hedgerow in which bryony had grown luxuriantly – and innocuously – for many years. Neither the farmer nor the workmen recog-

*White bryony
climbing through a
churchyard yew,
Oxfordshire.*

nised the roots, nor realised they were poisonous. Forty milking cows were turned into the field the morning after the work had been finished. By the afternoon four were dead, and post-mortems showed that each had eaten more than 4 lb of root. Curiously, as has been reported with other cases of bryony poisoning, two other animals which had eaten roots but survived developed a craving for the plant, 'and during the following summer, searched the hedgerows for it and ate leaves, stem and flowers, whenever they were available. This caused attacks of acute indigestion and diarrhoea with almost complete, but temporary cessation of milk secretion.'[9]

In rural France, there was a popular belief that bryony root would stop or slow down milk production in humans, too, and there used to be frequent cases of poisoning amongst weaning mothers. In this country the uses of the plant in folk-medicine were generally more cautious. Very small portions of the root were taken as a purgative or, distilled, as an external treatment for sunburn, boils, whitlows and other skin eruptions.[10]

The most bizarre use, which probably continued until the start of the eighteenth century, was in the construction of fake mandrake roots. Mandrake (*Mandragora autumnalis*) is a nightshade, and, like other members of the family, was anciently employed as a pain-killer and narcotic. The roots were also believed to have powerful magical and aphrodisiac properties (and, incidentally, to shriek when they were pulled out of the ground) because they occasionally grew in the rough shape of a human figure. Women would wear them round their necks or waists to help them conceive.

Since true mandrake is a native of the Mediterranean and hard to cultivate in Britain, the market was wide open for counterfeiters, who would carve out humanoid figures from any convenient root (bryony was the favourite), sometimes planting grass seeds in the root to grow into 'hair' (echoing the hair-roots of the true mandrake). John Baptista Porta described exactly how it was done by 'couzeners and conycatchers': 'You must get a great root of bryony, or wild nep, and with a sharp instrument engrave in it a man or a woman, giving either of them their genitories: then make holes with a puncheon into those places where the hairs are wont to

White bryony painted in an almost medieval arrangement by one of the Cliffords of Frampton in 1846.

grow, and put into those holes millet, or some other such thing which may shoot out his roots like the hairs of one's head. And when you have digged a little pit for it in the ground, you must let it lie there, until such time as it shall be covered with a bark, and the roots also be shot forth.' [11]

For all its dangerous and dubious history, white bryony is one of the most attractive ornaments of hedgerows and wood margins in the south and east of England, especially in deep winter, when the berries have been glazed by frost: 'I lately indulged a long held desire: to drape a vine of bryony berries round my neck. The flaming beads had always held this temptation for me, but, of course, as a child I was forbidden to touch poisonous berries.' [12]

Dog's mercury, *Mercurialis perennis* (VN: Boggard posy). Dog's mercury is a common woodland plant, whose spear-shaped leaves and spikes of small, greenish flowers are vaguely similar to those of some members of the *Chenopodium* family – the 'true' mercuries (see p. 22). But *Mercurialis* is highly poisonous; hence it became the 'bad', 'false' or 'dog's' mercury.

Given dog's mercury's usual habitat, its bright green, rather than mealy foliage, and a host of other differences, it is hard to see how the two kinds could be confused. But mistakes are made, even by modern foragers equipped with field guides. In 1983, the *British Medical Journal* published an account of a couple who ate a large quantity of dog's mercury in the belief that it was brooklime, an edible plant of the speedwell family (which at least bears more resemblance to it than any of the *Chenopodiaceae*). Four hours later they were admitted to hospital with vomiting, pain and gastric and kidney inflammation, and what their doctors described as a 'curious malar erythema' (reddening of the cheeks and jaw). Fortunately, after supportive treatment, both patients made a full recovery.[13]

Their doctors could find no record of malar erythema in the previous human cases (happily few) of poisoning by dog's mercury. But it was noted in what is probably the first account of the plant's toxic effects, in Shropshire in the spring of 1693:

'About Three Weeks ago, the Woman [wife of W. Matthews] went into the Fields and gathered some Herbs, and (having first Boyled them) Fryed them with Bacon for her own and her Families Supper: After they had been about Two Howrs in Bed, one of the Children (which is Dumb and about Seven Years Old) fell very Sick, and so did the other Two presently after; which obliged the Man and his Wife to Rise and take the Children to the Fire, where they Vomited and Purged, and within half an Hour fell fast asleep. They took the Children to bed as they were asleep, and they themselves went to bed too, and fell faster asleep too than ever they had done before. The Man waked next Morning about Three Hours after his usual Time, went to his Labour at Mr. *Newports*, and so by the strength of his constitution carried it off; but he says, he thought his Chin had bin all the Day in a Fire, and was forced to keep his Hat full of Water by him all the Day long, and frequently dipt his Chin in it as he was at his Work.'[14]

Dog's mercury often carpets the ground in old ashwoods.

In this instance one of the children died, after four days of unconsciousness – a grim warning against eating wild plants without being certain of their identity.

Dog's mercury is a problem plant in another way. It can grow in such dense, leafy colonies in woods that it shades out other, more light-demanding, species, such as oxlip, fly orchid and even young ash seedlings.[15] And, though it is predominantly a plant of ancient woods and old hedgerows, it can colonise new deciduous woodland at a rate of more than three feet a year, particularly where the soil is calcareous and dry. Mercury spreads by underground rhizomes, forming large 'clonal' patches in which all the stems share some peculiarity of leaf size, shape or tint. Some clones appear to be almost evergreen in their capacity to retain leaves through the winter.

Currently, dog's mercury appears to be going through a period of expansion in some areas of Britain, in the boulder-clay woodlands of East Anglia, for instance.[16] Colonies are growing in extent, and are composed of larger plants. Whether this is due to increasing shade in woods where coppicing or thinning has declined (which favours mercury's early leafing), or is a response to, say, some chemical changes in rainwater, it is hard to say.

Deadly nightshade, *Atropa belladonna* (VN: Dwale). Deadly nightshade is a handsome plant whose appearance belies its toxicity. It is a bushy perennial, growing up from ground level each year, its multiple branches carrying pale green, ribbed leaves. The flowers are purplish-brown bells, inside which the berries form – green at first, then a shiny black. They look as succulent and seductive as cherries, yet as few as three have been fatal to children. All parts of the plant contain quite high quantities of hyoscyamine (but very little atropine, contrary to popular belief and the suggestion in the scientific name), which acts in ways described above. Anne Pratt reported, somewhat improbably, that 'paralysis of the hand is said, on good authority, to have arisen from carrying it for some length of time'.[17]

Extracts of the plant are still used in stomach sedatives, and in tinctures for dilating the pupil of the eye. This is an ancient practice, and believed to be the origin of the Latin name 'belladonna'. Italian women used water distilled from the 'beautiful lady herb' as a cosmetic, to enlarge their pupils.

The tempting, cherry-like, but poisonous berries of deadly nightshade.

A useful plant, then, but one that landowners such as the National Trust are chary of tolerating, at least close to footpaths and car parks. But the disturbed soil in such places is precisely where deadly nightshade flourishes. On chalky and limestone soils (the only sites where it is native) it relishes rabbit warrens, old quarries and new forest tracks. After the great storm of 1987, large numbers of deadly nightshade plants sprang up – presumably from long-buried seed – in the root-holes of windthrown beeches in both the Chilterns and the South Downs.

Its frequent and somewhat sinister liking for graveyards (it grows directly out of tombs at St Cross, Holywell, in Oxford) is more curious.[18] Perhaps in such places it is a relic of ancient herbal cultivation, which was sometimes carried out at the edges of churchyards. A physic garden was almost certainly the source of the colony which grew at Guy's Hospital, London, until it was destroyed by building works in 1978.[19] And there have always been so many plants among the ruins of Furness Abbey in Lancashire, that the area is known as the Vale of the Deadly Nightshade.[20] This is a name which goes back at least to Wordsworth's day. He knew it as 'Bekang's Ghyll – or the dell of the Nightshade – in which stand St Mary's Abbey in Low Furness'.[21] In Felixstowe there are a number of sites of a variety with very pale lilac flowers, which may be a relic of an introduction by the Romans, who had a garrison in the old town. (The Suffolk botanist Francis Simpson used to remove the berries from these plants, to avoid their being 'found by some overzealous person and destroyed'.)[22]

Henbane is a casual that occasionally crops up on disturbed chalk grassland – as here, at Lulworth, Dorset.

Henbane, *Hyoscyamus niger*, is a sinister, malodorous species that even those with no knowledge of plants might suspect of being poisonous. The leaves are grey-green and densely covered with sticky hairs, the flowers liverish-looking, their pale yellow petals netted with purple veins.

Henbane contains considerable quantities of hyoscyamine and hyoscine, and was the poison with which Dr Crippen chose to murder his wife in 1910. Much earlier, it was prescribed as a specific remedy for toothache, because of a strong resemblance between the seed-heads and a row of molars. It certainly would have dulled the pain, but not the sufferers' imaginations, and Gerard describes how the hallucinatory effects of henbane were exploited by quack herbalists to bolster its reputation: 'The seede is vsed of mountibancke toothdrawers which runne about the countrey, for to cause woormes come foorth of mens teeth by burning it in a chafing dish with coles, the partie holding his mouth ouer the fume thereof: but some craftie companions to gaine money conuey small lute strings into the water, perswading the patient that those small creeping beasts came out of his mouth or other parts, which he intended to ease.'[23]

Henbane is native in sandy places by the sea, and on disturbed areas (rabbit warrens, for instance) on the chalk. Elsewhere it is a casual (as with the specimen that grew close to London's Festival Hall in 1966), or a relic of cultivation for medicinal uses. Long-dormant seed was almost certainly the origin of the many hundreds of plants which appeared in the summer of 1993 on set-aside land at Shrewton on Salisbury Plain.[24]

Thorn-apple, *Datura stramonium* (VN: Jimsonweed). By far the most dramatic of the family to appear in Britain, thorn-apple is a hefty, thick-stemmed annual from warmer regions, with large jagged leaves. And, like other *Datura* species, it has graceful, swan-necked white or purple flowers. The problem lies in the fruits, which are sufficiently like conkers to have attracted the interest of some children (though one specimen in a South Humberside garden was mistaken for a teasel).[25] But their formidable spines and nauseating smell must deter all but the most adventurous from exploring them more intimately, and there have been very few cases of human poisoning.

Thorn-apple's conker-like seed-cases are preceded by white swan-necked flowers.

The atmosphere of suspicion stirred up by the giant hogweed scare in the 1970s soon spread, however, to unfamiliar nightshades, especially on public land: 'Hard on the heels of the giant hogweed reported in August Rail News, comes another rare and dangerous plant – the thorn apple. It was spotted at New Milton [Hampshire] station by a retired chemist and local botanist. He told his next-door neighbour, one of Waterloo's assistants. Apparently the drug stramonium, which came from the plant, was once used for the alleviation of asthma. And it is believed wizards in medieval times used it. New Milton's Stationmaster was told that the plant was in his station car park and arranged for it to be destroyed. After hacking down the three-foot plant they dug up its roots and burned the lot.'[26]

British Rail's staff were probably erring on the side of caution, but they had some of the facts about the plant correct. It was used by herbal 'wizards' (though not medieval ones: it didn't arrive in this country until the late sixteenth century) – and perhaps 'witches', too. At the end of the seventeenth century John Pechey maintained that 'Wenches give half a dram of it to their Lovers, in beer or wine. Some are so skill'd in dosing of it, that they can make men mad for as many hours as they please.'[27]

And 'stramonium' extracted from the flowers and leaves (again, a mixture of nightshade family alkaloids such as atropine and hyoscine) had an honourable place in the treatment of asthma up to the end of the Second World War. Although some was grown commercially in this country, the bulk of our supplies had been imported from eastern Europe and were cut off in 1939. Wild specimens became valuable then, and the County Herb Committees were asked to gather leaves and flowers to augment the increased production from farms.

These days many thorn-apples originate from impurities in bags of South American fertiliser. But some could be relics of the days when the plant was more widely grown in this country. The 500 or so seeds which are scattered when the spiny capsule breaks open can stay dormant for exceptionally long periods. At the end of the nineteenth century, for example, occasional plants were seen at Woolwich Arsenal in London. When the eastern end was demolished before the building of Thamesmead in 1969, hundreds of thorn-apples reappeared in the churned-up soil. And when a local botanist found a plant on Wimbledon Common in 1935, he dismissed it as a casual, but it had been seen near the windmill on the same site a century before.[28] Hot summers (like 1975 and 1976) always produce a rash of records, often from suburban gardens.

A rich hunting ground for all manner of *Datura* species and other *Solanaceae* is proving to be the campus of Nottingham University. Here the Department of Pharmaceutical Sciences has for some years been investigating the medicinal properties of alkaloids from the nightshade family, which has involved the cultivation of live plant material for analysis and breeding. Over the past few years a remarkable number of these species have found their way into waste ground and cultivated beds on the campus, including six exotic *Solanum* species, five *Datura* species (and some spontaneous hybrids) and the aggressive South American sprawler **cock's-eggs**, *Salpichroa origanifolia*, with its pineapple-scented fruit.[29]

Vervain, *Verbena officinalis* (VN: The Herb). A rather local perennial of bare ground and rough grassland, chiefly on chalky soils in southern England, vervain was once a venerated plant, valued not just as a panacea (it was trum-

Vervain, an unprepossessing plant, but one of the Anglo-Saxons' most valued herbs.

peted as a cure for the plague in the Middle Ages) but as a magical charm, which could both protect against witches and demons and conjure up devilry of its own. It was traditionally associated with the gods of war, and gun-flints were sometimes boiled with rue and vervain to make them more effective.[30] As so often, the church exorcised its magic by appropriating the plant and suggesting that it grew under the cross at Calvary – though there were still incantations

143

for picking it, albeit couched in Christian language and symbolism:

Hallowed be thou, Vervein, as thou growest in the ground,
For in the mount of calvary there thou wast first found.
Thou healedst our Saviour Jesus Christ, and stanchedst his
    bleeding wound;
In the name of the Father, the Son, and the Holy Ghost,
    I take thee from the ground.[31]

The Isle of Man is the last British redoubt of belief in vervain's potency, though the plant is probably not native there:
'The Manx name, Yn Lus or Yn Ard Lus, gives an insight into its importance; the translation is The Herb or The Chief Herb. It has medical uses, but mere possession of it conferred all manner of protection. A person going on a journey would carry a piece, and many a Manxman would have a piece permanently sewn into his clothing. I have seen a number of plants growing in gardens, but so far I have not been successful in obtaining a plant for myself. The procedure for getting a piece is rather complicated. It cannot be asked for directly. Broad hints will be dropped and perhaps the possessor will take the hint and a plant will discreetly change hands, usually wrapped in paper. No word should be exchanged. It must always change hands from man to woman or vice-versa. It can be stolen, but I have not stooped to that yet.'[32]
The odd thing is that the plant behind this great edifice of lore is rather scrawny and nondescript. But its small pale lilac flowers, slowly opening up the spike until there is just a single one at the tip, suggested the nickname 'sparklers' to one family.[33]

Foxglove, *Digitalis purpurea* (VN: Fairy gloves, Fairy bells, Floppy dock, Tod-tails). The tapered, tubular flowers of foxglove obviously suggest the gloves of some small creature. But why, given their rosy-pink colouring, should it be a fox? (The name is not, as has sometimes been suggested, a contraction of folk's – i.e. fairies' – gloves: its root in Old English is clearly *foxes glofa*.) Perhaps it is because it grows in foxy places: amongst the bracken at the edges of heaths, on steep banks above rabbit-fields, by tracks up rough hill-

Foxgloves, source of the important heart drug digitalis.

144

pastures, in glades in acid woods. It defines, too, a particular moment of the year – the end of spring and beginning of high summer, when the landscape first begins to have a spent, tawny look.

Children, never pedantic about such things, have turned the fox's gloves into their own dolls, finger puppets and fake claws:

'The flowers were put on the finger tips, the point where they had been attached to the stalk forming a kind of hook so that the hands could then be used as pretend claws. To make the fingertip claws stay on, their size had to be carefully matched to the finger concerned.'[34]

'My mother, who was born in Derwen in Clwyd, used to "pop" foxgloves. To do this you remove a not fully opened trumpet and hold each end tightly with your thumbs to make an air-sac; then make it pop by pressing your thumbs together quickly.'[35]

The foxglove was also once widely used in folk-medicine, despite its high toxicity. Infusions of the leaves were given for sore throats and catarrh, and compresses for ulcers, swellings and bruises. But it was most frequently employed as a diuretic against dropsy (accumulation of fluid in the tissues), for which it could be dramatically but unpredictably effective, sometimes, alas, proving fatal. Ironically, it was the investigation of this powerful herb in the eighteenth century by the botanist and physician William Withering that was the turning point in the development of modern pharmacology and in its splitting away from traditional herbal medicine. Withering studied many cases of dropsy and its treatment by foxglove leaves, and he recorded his findings in his classic book, *An Account of the Foxglove* (1785).

He realised that its principal action was on the heart, whose beat it slowed and strengthened, which in turn stimulated the kidneys to clear the body and lungs of excess fluid. From this he found that the leaf could be an invaluable help in the treatment of heart failure. But the dosage was critical: a fraction too high and it could stop the heart altogether. Withering's insistence on the use of small and accurately measured quantities of dried foxglove leaf ('digitalis') led to a new discipline in the prescription of powerful plant drugs and eventually to the isolation and purification of the foxglove's active principles digitoxin and digoxin, still widely used in orthodox medicine as heart stimulants.

The drugs are now mostly prepared from imported leaves of European *Digitalis* species (usually *D. lanata*). But during the privation and blockades of the Second World War native foxglove leaves were gathered in large quantities by the County Herb Committees. These were mainly organised by the Women's Institutes, and a member of Bocking WI remembers that they used a condemned house for drying leaves, which were stretched out on netting in an upstairs room. In Montgomery a loft above a bakery was pressed into service and in Shrewsbury a clothes-drying room.[36]

In another part of Shropshire, wartime gathering revealed new sources for high-yield foxgloves: 'Foxglove was gathered in big quantities until about 1949 for the extraction of the heart drug digitalis. South Shropshire is divided diagonally by the high limestone ridge, Wenlock Edge. In many parts of this formation the surface limestone has been leached away, allowing the growth of the acid-loving foxglove. A drug manufacturer said that foxglove leaves from one site on top of the ridge were far richer in digitalis than any others known to him, British or foreign. His firm was very disappointed to learn of the small area involved.'[37]

But the old and sometimes reckless folk use of the leaves has never entirely disappeared. A GP in Oundle recalls that, when he was a houseman, he was called to examine a man treated by a herb-woman living in a wood in Repton, who had been given digitalis tea for breathlessness and was eating the 'tea-leaves' in sandwiches.[38]

Foxglove, especially the quite frequent white-flowered form, has been taken into cultivation, but has not changed very much in the process. I have seen occasional freaks in wild populations, where the top tubes have fused into a single speckled pink sunflower.

Dwarf elder, *S. ebulus* (VN: Danewort), is a non-woody perennial, often forming quite large colonies up to five feet tall, but dying away in winter. Its leaflets are long and lance-like, and have an unusual gravy-like smell when crushed. The flowers, which appear from July to late August, change from pink in bud to white with purplish anthers, developing eventually into black berries from September, by which time the foliage and stems of the plant have turned wine-red.

Perhaps these suffusions of purple and red helped bolster the legend that dwarf elder sprang from the blood of Danes slaughtered in battle. It is a curious legend, which probably originated from over-enthusiastic seventeenth- and eighteenth-century antiquarians misinterpreting the herbal name 'danewort', acquired because of dwarf elder's great effectiveness in producing the 'danes' or diarrhoea.[39] Although dwarf elder does grow at some historic sites, few have any connection whatsoever with Danes or battles. One Rutland contributor found that 'when I first moved into this area it was common knowledge locally that dwarf elder grew only where Danes had been buried after a skirmish with the Romano-British inhabitants'. But it proved to be literary folklore. The only one of the several colonies in the area at a remotely antiquarian site is on Oakham Castle Mound, where, with no great historical reverence, 'it has moved its position by 25 yards since I first saw it 30 years ago'.[40]

More typical sites for what may well have been an early herbal introduction from southern Europe are the unkempt hedge-banks round a chicken farm at Winterbourne Stoke, Wiltshire, and the enormous colonies, probably the largest in Britain, on railway embankments and waste ground at Stratford Marsh in east London. It occurs in a scatter of similarly marginal habitats across Britain.

But dwarf elder's capacity for generating spurious myths seems undiminished. In 1985, a Sussex writer pieced together, from a few suggestive quotes from old herbals and some scientific sleight-of-hand, an apparently serious account of how dwarf elder was used in the mass-production of Sussex dwarves for export to the courts of sixteenth-century Spain and Russia.[41]

Dwarf elder, or danewort, probably an early herbal introduction from southern Europe.

Source notes

SELECT BIBLIOGRAPHY

Dakers, Caroline, *The Countryside at War*, 1987

Davies, Jennifer, *The Wartime Kitchen Garden*, 1993

Evelyn, John, *Acetaria: A Discourse of Sallets*, 1699

Forsyth, A. A., *British Poisonous Plants*, 1968

Gerard, John, *The Herball*, 1597

Gibbons, Euell, *Stalking the Wild Asparagus*, 1962

Grigson, Geoffrey, *The Englishman's Flora*, 1955 and 1987

Grigson, Geoffrey, *A Herbal of All Sorts*, 1959

Hartley, Dorothy, *Made in England*, 1939

Hartley, Dorothy, *Food in England*, 1954

Mabey, Richard, *Food for Free*, 1972

Mabey, Richard, and Greenoak, Francesca, *Back to the Roots*, 1983

Ministry of Food, *Hedgerow Harvest*, 1943

White, Florence (ed.), *Good Things in England*, 1932

NOTES

Wild Greens

1 Gailann Keville-Evans, Shirley, Hants.

2 Eilert Ekwall, *The Concise Oxford Dictionary of English Place-names*, 4th edn, 1960

3 K. A. H. Cassels, Wimbish Green, Essex

4 Oliver Rackham, *Ancient Woodland*, 1980

5 Jack Oliver, Lockeridge, Wilts., in *BSBI News*, 63, 1993

6 Peter Marren; Mary Beith, Melness, Sutherland

7 Betty Don, Frampton Cotterell, Avon

8 Mark Powell, Riseley, Beds.

9 Antony Galton, Exeter, Devon

10 B. Johnson, Northwich, Ches.

11 D. C. Fargher, Port Erin, I. of M.

12 Christine Ashworth, Rochdale, Lancs.; also Philip Hodges, Ewloe Green, Clwyd

13 Sheila Llewellyn, Burcot, Oxon.

14 B. W. and M. Wilson, Ulverston, Cumb.

15 Margaret Bown, Lindfield, W. Susx

16 Grigson, 1955

17 Davies, 1993

18 Eilert Ekwall, *op. cit.*; also Margaret Gelling, *Place Names in the Landscape*, 1984

19 Milton Luby, The Hemp Patch, Shawbury, Shrops.

20 Grigson, 1955

21 Ian Hepburn, *Flowers of the Coast*, 1952

22 P. J. Spicer, Chichester, W. Susx

23 Roberta Blattner, Lewes, E. Susx

24 the late Jack Bishop, Blakeney, Norf.

25 'Plants, People, Places' project, Liverpool Museum

26 Judith Swarbrick, County Library, Preston, Lancs.

27 Mary Coote, Heacham, Norf.

28 Clive Stace, *New Flora of the British Isles*, 1991

29 Trevor Smith, Mytholmroyd, per Mrs Ellison, Mytholmroyd, W. Yorks.

30 A. Lee, Seascale, Cumb.

31 Thelma Farrer, Carlisle, Cumb.

32 Joan Nichols, Beetham, Cumb.

33 W. E. Foster, Epping, Essex

34 John Clare, *The Shepherd's Calendar*, Geoffrey Summerfield and Eric Robinson (eds), 1964

35 L. Clay, Paignton, Devon

36 White, 1932

37 Peggy Bridges, Bath, Avon

38 Julie Meech, Lower Broadheath, Worcs.

39 Eilert Ekwall, *op. cit.*

40 Evelyn, 1699

41 Mayhew, *London Labour and the London Poor*, 1851

42 Elizabeth Roy, Greatford, Lincs.

43 N. Morris, Andover, Hants.

44 William Turner, *The Names of Herbes*, 1548; Gerard, 1597

45 C. Pickett, Norfolk Society, Terrington St Clement, Norf.

46 Katherine Luto, London

47 Alexis Soyer, *The Culinary Campaign*, 1857

48 John Dony, *Flora of Hertfordshire*, 1967

49 Nick Sturt, West Wittering, W. Susx, in *BSBI News*, 58, 1991

50 John R. Palmer, South Darenth, Kent, in *BSBI News*, 66, 1994

51 C. P. Petch and E. L. Swann, *Flora of Norfolk*, 1968

52 Mrs Lloyd-Williams, per R. Lewis, Ty'n-y-groes, Gwyn.

53 H. G. B. Coast, Chatham, Kent

54 Gilbert White, *Journals*, Francesca Greenoak (ed.), 1986–89

55 Dr Larch Garrad, Manx Museum, Douglas, I. of M.

56 Mrs Gibson-Poole, High Salvington, W. Susx

57 Gilbert White, *op. cit.*

58 Nigel Mussett, Head of Biology, Giggleswick School, N. Yorks.
59 Mike Pratt, Cleveland Community Forest, Cleve.
60 Mary Hignett, Oswestry, Shrops.
61 Colin Jerry, Peel, I. of M.; Dr Larch Garrad, Manx Museum, I. of M.
62 Peter C. Horn, Kempstone, Beds.
63 R. A. Roberts, Ironbridge, Shrops.
64 Sir John Harington (trans.), *The Englishman's Doctor, or the School of Salerne*, 1607
65 Hilary Forster, Sedbury, Gwent
66 Mary Beith, Melness, Sutherland
67 William Sole, *Menthae Britannicae*, 1798
68 Margaret Evershed, Ewhurst, Surrey
69 Roy Genders, *The Scented Wild Flowers of Britain*, 1971
70 Vernon Rendall, *Wild Flowers in Literature*, 1934
71 Godfrey Nall, Shirley, W. Mids
72 John Keats, 'I Stood Tip-toe Upon a Little Hill', 1817
73 Children of Needham Market School, Suff.
74 Julia Upton, Youlgreave, Derby.
75 Margaret Evershed, Ewhurst, Surrey
76 C. J. Peat, Carlton, Warw.
77 Jack Boyce, Soham, Cambs.
78 Julia Sterling, Chelmondiston, Suff.
79 Mike Coyle, Stoke, Devon

Fruits

1 J. B. Foster, Arnside, Lancs.; also Richard Simon, Cullen, Banff.
2 O. L. Gilbert, 'Juniper in Upper Teesdale', in *Journal of Ecology*, 68, 1980,
3 Ian Findlay, National Nature Reserve Warden, Upper Teesdale, Durham
4 Jennifer Raven, Dorking, Surrey
5 John R. Akeroyd, Dereham, Norf., in *BSBI News*, 59, 1991
6 D. A. Ratcliffe (ed.), *A Nature Conservation Review*, 1977
7 Dr Brian Moffat, Fala Village, Lothian
8 Roy Vickery (ed.), *A Dictionary of Plant Lore*, 1995
9 Grigson, 1955
10 Wendy Morgans, Kington, Here.
11 Liza Goddard, Farnham, Surrey; Margaret Evershed, Ewhurst, Surrey; A. P. Mead, Kingston St Mary, Somer.
12 Robin Ravilious, Chulmleigh, Devon
13 T. T. Freeston, Wellington, Somer.
14 Colin Jerry, Peel, I. of M.
15 C. Walker, Condover, Shrops.
16 Janet Preshous, Lydham, Shrops.
17 S. A. Rippin, Fforest Coalpit, Gwent
18 E. Woolrich, Trentham, Staffs.
19 Richard Simon, Cullen, Banff.
20 Mabey and Greenoak, 1983
21 John Raven and Max Walters, *Mountain Flowers*, 1956
22 Jean Kington, Leyburn, N. Yorks.
23 Grigson, 1955
24 Richard Simon, Cullen, Banff.
25 Derek McLean, Stenton, E. Lothian
26 Mabey, 1972
27 Caroline and Peter Male, Halesowen, W. Mids
28 Dave Earl, Southport, 'Plants, People, Places' project, Liverpool Museum
29 Mr and Mrs Heard, Othery, Somer.
30 Ruth Ward, Culham, Oxon.
31 Kath Edwards, Bowdon, Ches.; Mrs N. Beresford, Bathley, Notts.
32 Hartley, 1954
33 *Evening Standard*, 8 October 1957
34 Jill Hill, Lower Peover, Ches.
35 Mike Palmer, 'Plants, People, Places', Liverpool Museum
36 Carol Bennett, Sprowston, Norf.
37 Simon Leatherdale, Forest Enterprise, Woodbridge, Suff.
38 Hilary Forster, Sedbury, Gwent
39 Hilda Evans, New Tredegar, Gwent
40 Dorothy Gibson, Tunstall, Lancs.
41 Gilbert White, *Journals*, Francesca Greenoak (ed.), 1986–89
42 Jill Lucas, Fixby, W. Yorks.
43 Ruth Ward, Culham, Oxon.
44 Roy Fussell, Chirton, Wilts.
45 Gerard, 1597
46 Dorothy Hinchclife, Murton, Cumbria, quoted in Davies, 1993
47 Dr Diane Bannister, Senior Information Officer, Boots Contract Manufacturing, Nottingham
48 Ministry of Food, 1943
49 Elizabeth Mellor, Haverhill, Suff.; S. Robson, Ripley, Surrey
50 J. N. Rounce, Great Walsingham, Norf.
51 Colin McLeod, Dundee
52 William Cobbett, *The Woodlands*, 1825
53 Pamela Michael, Lostwithiel, Corn.
54 Jack Oliver, Lockeridge, Wilts.
55 Mark Powell, Riseley, Beds.
56 Hazel Brecknell, Quarndon, Derby.
57 Edith Boxall, Handcross WI, per Janet Masters, Nymans, W. Susx
58 Jonathan and Wendy Cox, Kingston St Mary, Somer.

59 H. G. B. Coast, Chatham, Kent
60 Ray Tabor, Hundon, Suff.
61 L. J. Day, Harlow, Essex; also Cherry
    Chapman, Great Yeldham, Essex
62 Anne Proctor, Edlesborough, Beds.
63 Hamish Eaton, Weston Turville, Bucks.
64 Sue Benwell, Weston Turville, Bucks.
65 E. Woolrich, Trentham, Staffs.; also
    G. Greaves, Eccleshall, Staffs.
66 Peter Marren
67 Nigel Slater, 'On the damson trail', in
    Gardens Illustrated, August/September 1995
68 Oliver Rackham, *The History of the
    Countryside*, 1986
69 L. H. Grindon, *The Shakespere Flora*, 1883
70 Dorothy Hinchcliffe, Murton, Cumb.
71 A. Garfitt, Wells, Somer.
72 Grigson, 1955
73 Peter Marren
74 Gavin Maxwell, *Raven Seek Thy Brother*,
    1968
75 Dr Larch Garrad, Manx Museum, Douglas,
    I. of M.
76 Colin Jerry, Peel, I. of M.
77 Kenneth Jackson (ed.), *A Celtic Miscellany*,
    1971
78 C. P. Petch and E. L. Swann, *Flora of
    Norfolk*, 1968
79 Thomas Hale, *A Compleat Body of
    Husbandery*, 1756
80 John Evelyn, *Sylva, or a Discourse of Forest-
    trees*, 4th edn, 1706
81 Robert Chambers, *Popular Rhymes of
    Scotland*, 1847
82 Christine Ashworth, Rochdale, Lancs.
83 Barbara Penman, Hever, Kent
84 *Folklore*, 104, 1993
85 A. P. Mead, Kingston St Mary, Somer.
86 D. C. Fargher, Port Erin, I. of M.
87 Maura Hazelsdean, Crymych, Dyfed
88 T. J. Flemons, Luston, Here.
89 Joyce Dunkley, Market Harborough, Leic.
90 Duff Hart-Davis, *Independent*, 26 June
    1993
91 S. A. Rippin, Fforest Coalpit, Gwent
92 Lady Statham, Reigate, Surrey
93 Jane Belsey, Rock, Worcs.
94 Katrina Porteous, Beadnell, Northum.
95 F. H. Barratt, Cottingham, Humbs.
96 Colin Jerry, Peel, I. of M.
97 S. G. Terry, Yelverton, Devon
98 Alastair Scott, Forestry Commission,
    Edinburgh
99 Martin Spray, Ruardean, Glos.
100 G. H. Knight, 'Tree with a future', in
    Countryman Wildlife Book, 1969

Kitchen Medicines

1   Grigson, 1955
2   Gerard, 1597
3   Dr Sue Thompson, Hawstead, Suff.; Susan
    Cowdy, The Lee, Bucks.; Marion Dadds, The
    Lee, Bucks.; Helen Weidell, Newbury,
    Berks.; T. J. Flemons, Luston, Here.;
    Jacqueline Seaborn, Evesham, Worc.
4   David Wall, Lichfield, Staffs.
5   Nikolaus Pevsner, *The Leaves of Southwell*,
    1945
6   Gerard, 1597
7   Philip Henry Stanhope, 5th Earl Stanhope,
    Life of the Rt Hon. William Pitt, 1861–62
8   Ursula Bowlby, Ullinish, Isle of Skye
9   M. Haines, Linwood, Hants.
10 Margaret Gelling, *Place Names in the
    Landscape*, 1984
11 George Y., Stonegrave, N. Yorks.
12 M. J. Yates, Whitby Naturalists' Club,
    Saltburn, Cleve.
13 Penny Bennett, Littleborough, Lancs.
14 Mary Beith, Melness, Sutherland; also Bridie
    Pursey, Elphin, Sutherland
15 Kathleen MacLeod Rodger, Elphin,
    Sutherland
16 H. G. B. Coast, Chatham, Kent
17 Jo Darrah, Victoria & Albert Museum, per
    Maureen Patterson, Enfield, Middx; Margaret
    Pilkington, Lindfield, W. Susx
18 Pamela Michael, Lerryn, Lostwithiel, Corn.
19 Kevin and Susie White, Hexham, Northum.
20 Jane Arnold, Bishopstone, Wilts.
21 B. Phillips, Romsey, Hants.
22 Ian and Victoria Thomson, Bentworth,
    Hants.
23 Margaret Bown, Lindfield, W. Susx
24 Mrs Williamson, [n.a.]
25 Mark Powell, Riseley, Beds.
26 Dr Gavin Ewan, Aylesbury, Bucks.
27 R. Lewis, Ty'n-y-groes, Gwyn.
28 Peter Crossland, Upper Denby, W. Yorks.
29 Alice Payton, via her daughter Helen Turner,
    Goring-on-Thames, Berks.
30 K. Copestake, The Grange Rest Home,
    Staffs.; Kathleen Simpson, Wilmslow, Ches.
31 C. Coiffait, Welton, Humbs.
32 Norma de Smet, Isfield, E. Susx
33 Mark Powell, Riseley, Beds.
34 E. S. Johnson *et al.*, 'Efficacy of feverfew as
    prophylactic treatment of migraine', in
    British Medical Journal, 31 August 1985
35 J. Farrow, Martham, Norf.; Anne Fowler,
    Llanbedr, Gwyn.
36 Dr J. D. S. Birks, Malvern, Worcs.

37 Sue Thompson, Hawstead, Suff.
38 Thomas Hill, *The Gardeners Labyrinth*, 1577 (edited with an introduction by Richard Mabey, 1987 and 1988)
39 Heather R. Winship, 'Chamomile – The herb of humility in demise', in *British Wildlife*, 5(3), 1994
40 A. P. Mead, Kingston St Mary, Somer.
41 Margaret Lovel Graham, Headley, Hants.
42 R. M. Wickenden, Staplecross, E. Susx

Banes and Baubles

1 Primrose Warburg, Oxford, Oxon.
2 Kevin and Susie White, Hexham, Northum.
3 Brian Moffat, Soutra, Lothian
4 *Guardian*, 13 September 1993; Stuart Carpenter, Bishops Stortford, Herts.; Pooran Desai, Bioregional Development Group, Carshalton, Surrey
5 Madeline Reader, Horney Common, E. Susx; C. A. Sinker *et al.*, *Ecological Flora of the Shropshire Region*, 1985 and 1991
6 Kevin and Susie White, Hexham, Northum.
7 Roy Fussell, Chirton, Wilts.
8 Frank Penfold, Arundel, W. Susx, in *Sussex Trust Newsletter*
9 Forsyth, 1968
10 Anne Pratt, *The Poisonous, Noxious and Suspected Plants of Our Fields and Woods*, 1857
11 John Baptista Porta, *Natural Magick*, 1558
12 Caroline Male, Halesowen, W. Mids
13 F. Rugman *et al.*, '*Mercurialis perennis* (dog's mercury) poisoning: a case of mistaken identity', in *British Medical Journal*, 287, 24–31 December, 1983
14 'Part of a Letter from Mr. T. M. in Salop, to Mr. William Baxter, concerning the strange effects from the eating Dog-mercury ...', in *Philosophical Transactions of the Royal Society*, 203, VIII, September 1693
15 Oliver Rackham, *Ancient Woodland*, 1980
16 Trevor James, Hertfordshire Environmental Records Centre, Hitchin
17 Anne Pratt, *op. cit.*
18 Roy Maycock, Milton Keynes, Bucks.
19 Rodney M. Burton, *Flora of the London Area*, 1983
20 Doris Page, Barrow-in-Furness, now of Victoria, British Columbia
21 In a note to the poem 'To the Lady Fleming', composed 1823
22 Francis Simpson, *Simpson's Flora of Suffolk*, 1982
23 Gerard, 1597

24 Barbara Last, Berwick St James, Wilts.
25 S. H. R. Jackson, Broughton, Humbs.
26 *Rail News*, October 1970
27 John Pechey, *The Compleat Herbal of Physical Plants*, 1694
28 Rodney M. Burton, *op. cit.*
29 Julian M. H. Shaw and Belma Konuklugil, Dept of Pharmaceutical Sciences, Nottingham University, in *BSBI News*, 65, 1994
30 Richard Folkard, *Plant Lore*, 1892
31 John White, *The Way to the True Church*, 1608
32 Colin Jerry, Peel, I. of M.
33 Francesca Greenoak, Wigginton, Herts.
34 Hazel Sumner, St Weonards, Here.
35 Gwen Redshaw, Rhewl, Clwyd; also Diana Harding, Dulverton, Somer.
36 Davies, 1993
37 T. J. Flemon, Luston, Here.
38 per Northamptonshire Wildlife Trust, Oundle Branch
39 John Parkinson, *Theatrum Botanicum*, 1640
40 K. G. Messenger, Uppingham, Leic.
41 *Sussex Life*, January 1985

Acknowledgements

To the Countryside Commission, English Nature, the Ernest Cook Trust and Reed Books for so generously supporting the research stage of the project.

To Common Ground – and Sue Clifford and Angela King especially – who acted as charitable host to the project and who were unfailing in their support and encouragement whenever my own enthusiasm showed signs of wilting. And to Daniel Keech and John Newton, who worked as full-time information and research officers, principally from Common Ground's office, but who also did invaluable and original fieldwork beyond the call of duty.

To Peter Marren, James Robertson and Ruth Ward, who co-ordinated research for us in Scotland, Wales and Oxfordshire respectively.

To Roz Kidman Cox, editor of *BBC Wildlife* Magazine, and Patrick Flavelle, producer of BBC TV's *CountryFile*, who gave us space and time (and encouragement) to recruit contributors.

To the many societies and associations, national, regional and local, whose members and staff were amongst the principal contributors:

Botanical Society of the British Isles, British Bryological Association, British Association for Nature Conservation, British Naturalists' Association, British Trust for Conservation Volunteers, Butterfly Conservation Society, Churchyard Conservation Project, John Clare Society, Council for Protection of Rural England, Countryside Council for Wales, Folklore Society, Forest Enterprise, Help the Aged, Herb Society, Learning through Landscapes, Local Agenda 21, National Association for Environmental Education, National Association of Field Studies Officers, National Farmers' Union Scotland, National Federation of Women's Institutes, National Trust, Open Spaces Society, Plantlife, Poetry Society, Ramblers' Association, the Royal Botanic Gardens at Kew and Edinburgh, Royal Forestry Society, Royal Society for Nature Conservation, Scottish Environmental Education Council, Scottish Natural Heritage, Tree Council and the Parish Tree Wardens network, Watch, Youth Hostels Association.

Arthur Rank Centre, Association of Leicestershire Botanical Artists, Bioregional Development Group, Bolton Museum, Cheshire Landscape Trust, Cleveland Community Forest, Cobtree Museum, the County Wildlife Trusts of: Berkshire, Buckinghamshire and Oxfordshire; Cambridge and Bedfordshire; Cleveland; Cornwall; Derbyshire; Gloucestershire; Hampshire and Isle of Wight; Hertfordshire and Middlesex; Kent; Lancashire; London; Norfolk; Northamptonshire; North Wales; Nottinghamshire; Scotland; Suffolk; Surrey; Wiltshire. Cymdeithas Edward Llywd, Derbyshire Ranger Service, Deeside Leisure Centre, Flora of Dunbartonshire Project, Groundwork Trusts of Merthyr and Cynon, Kent Thames-side and Amber Valley, Humberside County Council Planning Department, Liverpool Museum, Manchester Herbarium, Mid-Yorkshire Chamber of Commerce, Montague Gallery, Norfolk Rural Life Museum, Norfolk Society, North York Moors National Park, Social and Education Training Norfolk, Ted Ellis Nature Reserve, South-east Arts, University of Sussex Centre for Continuing Education, Warwickshire Rural Community Council, Wildplant Design.

Boxley Parish Council, Bradford City Council Countryside Service, Buchan Countryside Group, Thomas Coram School, Cumbria Broadleaves, Dragon Environment Group, Embsay with Eastby Nature Reserve, Giggleswick School, Great Torrington Library, Greenfield Valley Heritage Centre, Mike Handyside Wildflowers, Harehough Craigs Action Group, Hedingham Heritage Group, Hexham Nursery, Horsham Natural History Society, Ingleby Greenhow Primary School, Graham Moore Landscape Works, Lee Parish Society, Little Wittenham Nature Reserve, Oakfield Methodist Church, Paulersbury Horticultural Society, Pytchley Parish Sunday School Group, St Mary's Church Kirk Bramwith, Spiral Arts, Wealden Team Conservation Volunteers, West Bromwich Albion Football Club, White Cliffs Countryside Management Project, Whitegate and Marton Parish Council.

My personal thanks for their support to Charles Clark, Gren Lucas, Sir Ralph Verney and the late Sir William Wilkinson, and to the Leverhulme Trust for their generous award of a Research Fellowship to help fund my own researches.

To the friends and colleagues who gave me hospitality, company and much stimulating information during my own research trips: Elizabeth Roy and Nigel Ashby, Ronald Blythe, Hilary Catchpole and the pupils of Thomas Coram School, Berkhamsted, Rollo and Janie Clifford, David Cobham, Mike and Pooh Curtis, Roger Deakin, the late Edgar Milne-Redhead,

Robin and Rachel Hamilton, Anne Mallinson, Richard Simon, Jane Smart, Jonathan Spencer, Ian and Vicky Thomson. And to Liza Goddard, who acted as guinea-pig contributor whilst I was still refining the idea of the project and who accompanied me on some of the early field-trips, and to Pattie Barron for her patience.

To Penelope Hoare, my publisher at Sinclair-Stevenson, and the directors of Reed Books, who gave unflagging support to the project over what, in the modern book world, was a very long gestation period.

To Robin MacIntosh, my personal assistant, who helped in so many ways, especially with the awesome task of putting the contributions into some order. To Vivien Green, my agent, especially for bolstering me up during the low periods of the writing. To Douglas Matthews, for the speed and accuracy with which he produced the indexes. To Philip Oswald, whose vast background knowledge and meticulous attention to detail not only gave the text botanical respectability but added a wealth of anecdotes, historical notes and stylistic improvements. And to Roger Cazalet, my editor, for his diligence, dedication, patience and care.

And finally, the warm thanks of all of us go to the many thousands of people who contributed to *Flora Britannica* and without whom it would not exist. Those of you whose stories and notes have found their way into the text are individually acknowledged in the Source notes. But every single contribution helped form the entries and the overall flavour of the book. Please keep contributing, as we hope that the first edition of *Flora Britannica* will not mark the end of the project so much as the beginning of a new phase.

Picture credits

Bob Gibbons: 6, 10-11, 12, 14, 18, 20, 22, 25, 27, 29, 33, 35, 37, 40-1, 43, 47, 48-9, 54, 59, 60-1, 62, 64, 67, 68, 70, 71, 73, 78, 79, 82, 88, 92-3, 95, 102-3, 109, 112-13, 117, 121, 124-5, 127, 128, 130, 138, 139, 141, 143, 145, 149.
Gareth Lovett Jones: frontispiece, 13, 17, 23, 31, 45, 85, 91, 98, 107, 115, 132, 136.
Bodleian Library: 75, 129.
Bridgeman Art Library, London: 56, 69.
Tony Evans © Timelapse Library: 51.
Marlborough Photographic Library: 80.
Royal Mail: 58.
Eddie Ryle-Hodges: 105, 134.

Index